From the Great Depression

To Millionaire

Family Tragedies – Poverty – World War II
Business Ventures – Estrangements

By
Sam S. Ruffalo

Publisher: Walworth Publishing Company LLC
Muskego, Wisconsin

Published by
Walworth Publishing Company, LLC
Muskego, Wisconsin in 2006
Printed in the United States of America

ISBN-13: 978-0-9787194-0-1
ISBN-10: 0-9787194-0-9

Library of Congress Control Number 2006929679

DEDICATION

This book was written in loving memory of my mother and father; especially my mother, for her love, devotion, kindness and patience in raising three spirited sons to be hard-working, conscientious men who never lost sight of the importance of family.

Table of Contents

Preface

As I neared the age of eighty-two, I could no longer deny that I was reaching the later years of my life as a father, grandfather, and perhaps a great-grandfather. I decided to write my memoir to explain fundamental truths for the benefit of my children and grandchildren, to foster a better understanding of their ancestors' lives.

As people age, they often look forward to spending time with their children and grandchildren, relating stories about their lives and those of their ancestors. When these tales cannot be voiced directly, a written account provides a lasting record where family members can seek their past when they are ready.

As children and grandchildren mature, they are bound to ask some day, "Who were my ancestors? Where did they come from? What did they do?" In my family, I am the link to the past. I hope my children and grandchildren will see the good times and the bad times about their ancestors. My memoir not only tells a story about my life, but also describes a time in history not experienced by most who are living today—before radios, televisions, computers, e-mails, cell phones, and VCRs and DVDs. I hope as a result of reading this book that my loved ones will better understand the role we all play in the lives of others. This information can be passed to our future generations so they will know and honor their ancestors.

This book does not contain fiction. The dates, events, actions, and their outcomes have been accurately and faithfully recounted based on my own recollections, discussions with relatives and friends, and research into personal and registered records.

Conversations presented in dialogue form are based upon my memory of these events but are not intended to represent word for word statements. They are intended to convey the significant meaning and spirit of the words spoken.

Acknowledgments

I extend my deepest gratitude to those who helped me to write my story. I'm profoundly grateful to my loving cousin Eleanora (Chiappetta) Peterson, three years my senior; my lifelong friends Bob Chiapetta and his wife, Laura (Gagliardi); and Sam Caldario, my godfather's son and my friend since we were born. Many thanks to octogenarian Tony Maglio, a pillar in Milwaukee community activities of the past; Alfred Bartolini, a boyhood friend; Robert Holoubek, my shipmate in World War II and friend to this date; Karen and Keith Wiest, from the old neighborhood and my friends for forty-five years; and Kathy Liegler, whom I've known for fifty years.

I would not want to miss giving my thanks to Edward Caldario, a retired associate professor at the University of Illinois, whom I have known since our first words. I thank him his help with the facts he personally remembers and those related by his mother in a tape recording of some of our history. Also not to be forgotten are my brother, Vince; Mary Duran, my wife's daughter; Louise Ruffalo, my sister-in-law; and Bob Chiapetta and his wife, Laura.

For their helpful assistance in the search for my World War II records, I would like to thank the National Archives and Records Administration (NARA) Northeast Region in New York City and NARA's Pacific Alaska Region, in Seattle, Washington, for copies of the log pages from the ships on which I sailed. Their care and attention to my request is greatly appreciated.

My gratitude also to Melanie Rigney, my book's editor and the former editor of *Writer's Digest*, for her patience and generous assistance in helping me tell my story with expressions of life's joys, sadness, and disappointments.

My special gratitude and appreciation to Mary Hensel, daughter of friends Karen and Keith Wiest, for using her mass communication training to provide me with guidance and literary assistance.

Last but most important, I extend my most heartfelt thanks to my wife, Betty, for her endless patience while reading though numerous manuscript drafts, and serving as my constant sounding board during the many months it has taken me to write this book.

Chapter 1: In the Beginning

My Parents Emigrate from Italy to Chicago's South Side

My father, Gaspare Ruffalo, was born January 17, 1891, in Rende, which is in the Italian province of Cosenza and the region of Calabria. My mother, Concetta (Chiappetta) Ruffalo, was born December 8, 1894, in Rende. They were married in Marano Marchesato, a town in Cosenza, on December 12, 1912. Dad was twenty-one and Mom was eighteen.

Calabria is located in the lowest southeastern tip of Italy. It is approximately fifty miles wide and almost two hundred miles long and forms the lower part of Italy, sometimes referred to as the boot.

In Italy, my mother and father worked as farm laborers on their parents' farms in Rende, located in the mountains. My parents left Italy because they wanted a better way of life and had learned from people who had left before them that America offered such opportunities. Many of their friends had the same dream. My parents and some of their friends came to America, settled in Chicago, and maintained their friendships for the rest of their lives.

My father arrived at Ellis Island in New York on May 27, 1914; my mother followed seven years later on October 4, 1921. She worked on her parents' farm and raised my brother Serafino until my father had enough money to pay for her voyage. Serafino was my parents' third child born in Italy. Mom lost one child in a miscarriage; another died of pneumonia shortly after being born. During this time, she shared time with her nearby lady friends who also eventually came to America.

Immigration officials misspelled many immigrant names. My parents didn't speak any English until months after their arrival and didn't read or write English or Italian. My father's passenger record shows his last name as Ruffalo, but on my mother's record and their marriage certificate, it is Ruffolo. As it has turned out, our family's last name became known as Ruffalo. I always say now, "It's 'Ruffalo,' just like buffalo, but only with an 'R.'"

In addition to accumulating money for my mother's and Serafino's voyage, my father had to save for their train fare from New York to Chicago, where he was living. He also saved for unforeseen emergency needs, and to pay for food and rent. He worked hard and long hours in Chicago's sweatshops as an unskilled laborer. I think he also shoveled coal into factory furnaces. He often worked fourteen hours per day, six days per week. I do not know how much he earned or where he worked, but he had a reputation among our relatives and friends as a hard worker and a respected individual. My parents never discussed with me their happiness and celebration in being together again after they had been separated for seven years. Mom did tell me later, when I was old enough to understand love, how much she loved my father as a fine man. She said that he loved her very much and that his eyes would sparkle when they were together.

They first lived in a rented apartment on the second floor in an old two-family dwelling on the South Side of Chicago, a tightly knit Italian community on South Princeton Avenue. Croatian immigrants lived nearby and attended the same neighborhood Catholic churches. The second floor had four sleeping rooms for seven boarders. To earn extra income, my mother washed their grimy, dirty work clothes.

My godfather's wife, Raffaela Caldario, who we also called my godmother, had a son named Sam too. Sam and I have been friends our whole lives. Our families lived in the front and back of the second floor and shared the same bathroom, each with our own door. I was instructed to be sure I closed the latch on the Caldarios' side of the door to let them know the bathroom was occupied.

In those days, women washed clothes by hand, back and forth on a scrub board. It was hard work. Eventually, wringers were invented that consisted of two rollers turned with a handle to squeeze out the water before the clothes were hung on a line to dry. Electric washing machines and electric wringers came on the scene later.

Hundreds, if not thousands, of Italians settled on the South Side of Chicago near Comiskey Park. Old houses, mostly two-story houses, were built close together. Children often played on the sidewalks and streets. Very few people owned automobiles then.

Men worked twelve or fourteen hours per day, and women worked hard at home. They cooked, washed clothes, cleaned the house, and took care of the children. They didn't have any of our modern appliances or conveniences, so domestic chores took much more time.

My parents were good friends with *Comare* (coh-MAH-ree, Italian for godmother) Raffaela, and her husband, *Compare* (cohm-PAH ree, godfather) Emilio Caldario, and Comare Luigina and her husband, Compare Charles (Charlie) Caldario. When addressing one another however, rather than use the formal title for the godparent relationship, we used the Italian word *coomba* for the men and *cooma*for the women. Charlie came to America long before his wife and their child, Edward, now called Ed. Coomba Charlie worked in a bakery and often gave us a fresh coffee cake for breakfast.

Because at least one of the adults served as a godparent for one of the children in our respective families, we all referred to the adults as coomba or cooma. We were taught that a godparent relationship was of the highest order, next to a natural father or mother relationship to a child, due to a commitment to take care of their godchild if both parents passed away.

I remember good times with Compares Emilio and Charlie, and Comares Raffaela and Luigina while we lived in Chicago. I especially recall our dozens of get-togethers and hearing the adults sharing laughter and merriment. Most of the adults came from the Cosenza area, so they had much in common. My brothers and I have been lifelong friends with our godparents and all of their children: this includes Ed, who came from Italy as a child, and his sister Edith, born in Chicago, children of Comare Luigina and Compare Charlie; and Sam, Josephine, Sue, Frank, and Tom, all born in Chicago, children of Comare Raffaela and Compare Emilio. We shared our first communions, confirmations, marriages, and funerals.

An Accident Takes My Brother Serafino

For my mother, the saddest event of her life was the death of Serafino in 1924. He was just ten years old. She witnessed this sudden and terrifying accident through her second-floor kitchen window. She saw a yellow taxicab swiftly moving toward Serafino as he was crossing the street. There was no escape. He died upon impact. She described her frantic impulse to jump out of the window to get to her son and try to save his life. She held back, remembering that she was six months pregnant. That unborn child was me.

I can still recall Serafino's picture as he lay in his casket dressed in a suit. It was on our walls for several years. I don't recall ever seeing any pictures of Serafino taken before he died. Photos in those days were taken only at a studio, and only rarely. I felt sadness and pain in my heart for the suffering I know my mother experienced due to this tragic event.

My Brothers, Emil and Vincent, and I Are Born

I was born at home on South Princeton Avenue in Chicago on June 18, 1924. I was named as Serafino on my birth certificate. However, I was always called Sam.

My brother Emil was born in the 2800 block on South Wells Street in Chicago on September 13, 1926, very near where I was born. He was named Umile on his birth certificate. We called him Emil ("Ay-mil") all his life.

My brother Vincent was born on February 4, 1930, also in Chicago. His birth certificate showed he was named Vicenzo. For many years, we called him Jim. Later, Jim preferred Vincent or Vince, the English version of Vicenzo.

We were all baptized at the Santa Maria Incoronato at 218 Alexander Street, a Catholic church very near where we lived. My godfather was Emilio Caldario. We were very close. I visited him at least once or twice annually until he died in his nineties. My godmother's name was Mary Gertesiano, my mother's friend. I did not see her much or recall much about her.

Growing Up on the South Side

Our neighborhood was about four or five blocks from Comiskey Park in a tough part of Chicago. Between 1926 and 1932, our country continued to change. Radio was becoming accessible to middle-class families such as mine, although at forty dollars, a radio was twice the price of a decent wool suit. In early 1926, Al Capone became a notorious leader of Chicago gangsters and gave the city a strong criminal identity. The most heinous and spectacular mob hit in gangland history took place on Valentine's Day, February 14, 1929, in a warehouse located at 2122 North Clark Street, about four miles from our neighborhood. It is known in history as the St. Valentine's Day Massacre. Seven gangsters were killed by gunfire by other gangsters who posed as Chicago policemen. Capone was thought to be the one who ordered the shooting, but was in Florida at the time of the massacre.[1]

At the end of the 1926 baseball season, Comiskey Park was expanded; the old wooden bleachers were replaced with a steel and concrete upper deck. Penicillin was discovered by 1929. The unemployment rate increased from 5.2 percent to more than 25 per-

---

[1] For more information, see www.prairieghosts.com/valentine.html.

cent by the 1930s, and a typical household income hovered around $1,500 per year. A loaf of bread from the corner store was a dime, and a new shiny car would cost you from $750 to $2,995, depending on the model.

We lived in this neighborhood until 1932. Famous thugs and gangsters frequented the area. Fortunately, my father, our godfathers and relatives, and my parents' friend Uncle Santo were never engaged in any criminal connections or illegal activities. We called Santo "Uncle Santo" because he was a close friend of relatives in Italy. I remember Uncle Santo would bring me a toy when he came to visit us.

When I use the word "godfather" in my story, it has absolutely no relationship to the Mafia. My brothers and I were not influenced by criminal activities nor were we arrested for any wrong-doings except for common traffic violations during our lifetimes.

I recall a dangerous experience I had: one day, while I was playing in the street—we did not have fields or playgrounds nearby—someone yelled at me, *"Get out of the street quick!"* I jumped, and when I turned around, one black car was chasing another black car down the street and shooting at it. Neither car was a police car. They hadn't missed me by much. They were gangsters, apparently in a war. Although I didn't know it then, I learned later that thugs were demanding "protection money" from our neighborhood's shopkeepers.

My favorite place to buy candy was a small grocery store at Twenty-Eighth and Princeton. It was popular and later became known as Tooty's Corner. It closed in 1998, after eighty-four years in business. Michael Maione's *Tooty's Corner* (Pentland Press, 1999) relates some of the troubles in the 1950s in the blocks surrounding this store. Jim Ritter, a staff writer for the *Chicago Sun-Times*, wrote an article titled "Tooty's Checks Out" for the July 6, 1998, issue. It gives a brief history of Tooty's store and the flavor of the times starting in 1922.

The Prohibition Years

These years during my childhood were also the years of Prohibition. I was surprised to learn much later in life that our landlady, who had two grown daughters, sold moonshine from her apartment just one floor below us. The liquor was called moonshine because allegedly it was sold at night while the moon was shining. I know for sure that my mother, father, and godparents never had anything to do with selling homemade wines or moonshine, also sometimes referred to as "white lightning."

My parents, like many of our Italian friends, did make their own wine for home consumption only. It was made with grapes of the grapevines in their backyards. A strong alcoholic drink called *grappa* was also occasionally made at home for personal use. The illegal sale of liquor flourished and encouraged criminal activities, formations of gangs, gang warfare, the growth of the Mafia and murders. Fortunately, prohibition was repealed in 1933 after thirteen years.

Chapter 2: The Great Depression Hits

Our first family portrait was taken at a studio in Chicago in 1928. My father was thirty-seven, my mother thirty-four. I was four and Emil was two. Our brother Vince had not yet been born. When friends and relatives looked at our family picture, I recall some of our friends saying that my brother and I looked like little angels. But were we? Not really! Later, I heard from some of our friends and relatives that we were little "devils." There's no doubt Emil and I were playful kids, Emil more so than I was. Everyone said so! When we both got into "trouble," I recall saying, "Ma, I didn't do it! Emil did it!" Emil often said the same thing about me when he got into "trouble." We also wrestled together at times. We continued to wrestle each other until thirteen or fourteen. We were brothers with great meaning to our relationship and love in our hearts and a strong family bond, a bond shared by our brother, Vince, born a few years later.

The Depression Affects Everyone

The Great Depression began on October 24, 1929. That day is known as "Black Thursday," the day the stock market crashed. Between October 29 and November 13, 1929, the day when stock prices hit their lowest point, over $30 billion "disappeared" from the American economy. This amount was comparable to the total amount of money that the federal government had spent to fight World War I. By 1933, 11,000 of the United States' 25,000 banks had failed; millions of people had lost their homes; and hundreds of thousands of men, women, and children roamed the cities and countryside looking for food, shelter, and work. The Great Depression did not officially "end" until 1941, when America entered into World War II.

I remember as a child hearing some people had jumped out of windows because the market had crashed. I recall being puzzled why people would jump out of windows simply because they lost money in the stock market. I thought, "How dumb! Over losing money?"

The market continued to fall and reached its lowest point in 1932. It was the worst economic slump ever experienced by the United States and affected all other countries in the industrialized world. The Depression seriously affected workers throughout the entire country.

My dad worked as a laborer in the foundry twelve to fourteen hours per day prior to the Depression. It was in this economic environmental setting that I grew up, and I recall many vivid childhood memories from these dark years. The Depression's effects will never leave my thoughts; they have left their mark on my memories and my life's philosophies.

I've seen the movie *Cinderella Man*—the story of fighter and folk hero Jim Braddock, who defeated heavyweight champ Max Baer in a fifteen-round slugfest in 1935—and believe it's as real as it can get when showing the Depression's effects. The family life, home scenes, and unemployment miseries shown were realistic, not at all exaggerated.

Air conditioners were unknown to us, as were refrigerators. In most kitchens, there was a wooden icebox with a shelf for ice and another for important foods such as milk, eggs, and meat (rare in those days). Trucks traveled up and down the streets to deliver ice. The iceman would carry the block of ice held with a large pair of tongs up the stairs, into our apartment, and place it in our icebox during the week as needed. While the iceman was inside, some of the bigger kids would jump onto a step in the back of the truck and take broken pieces of ice off the truck platform and eat it to cool off or just for plain enjoyment. I still remember the extreme heat of a Chicago summer. As young kids, running through the blasts of water from the open fire hydrants on our block was our only consistent relief. Summer nights were almost unbearable. We didn't have fans.

Chicago winters were just as brutal as the summers. For heat, we had a potbelly stove in our room next to the kitchen. We burned firewood. When it was time for a bath, my mother would place a large metal tub in the room and fill it with water she had boiled. We had few amenities during the cold winters of the early 1930s. After she finished washing Emil or me, we would step out on to the floor, and then she would wrap us with a towel to lessen our shivering. I can't say these were the "good old days."

After we moved from 2855 South Wells Street to 3022 South Wells Street, we became members of St. Jerome's Church. It is now called St. Lucy, and has remained at the same location. I also attended St. Jerome's School.

After attending St. Jerome's for a while, I attended Ward School, a public school in our neighborhood. I don't know why my parents moved us from St. Jerome's to Ward. I'm sure it wasn't because my teacher, a Catholic Nun, had placed me in the closet for a couple of hours. Parents favored and sided with the teachers in those days. I would guess my parents probably yelled at me for having been placed in the closet in the first place. My parents, as other parents, believed in discipline if children misbehaved in school or anywhere else. My godparents' children, Sam and Ed Caldario, also attended Ward. We've remained good friends throughout our lives.

Another good school friend of mine was named Roy. In 1932, my parents informed me that we were leaving Chicago to move to Kenosha, Wisconsin. I cried; I told them I didn't want to go. I explained I didn't want to go to school in Kenosha, because I would never see Roy again. I don't think my parents knew Roy's parents. After leaving Chicago, Roy and I lost touch. In those days, we didn't have cell phones or computers. We could've written letters, but, well, we were eight. I missed my Chicago friends, but I adapted quickly to my new surrounding and made new friends.

Heart Trouble

During my childhood, I was sick and bedridden fairly often. I also remember being told at four or five years old that I had kidney problems and a weak heart. A doctor came to our home to examine me at least twice. These were the days that doctors made house calls. I don't recall if I was taking medication. I do recall having to remain in bed.

When I was seven, I was placed in Jackson Sanitarium, now known as LaRabida Children's Hospital, which is located near Chicago's lakefront.[2] I was an in-patient there for four months. Later in life, I learned that Jackson Sanitarium admitted only children with rheumatic fever. Today, LaRabida is known to specialize in the treatment of children with tuberculosis.

I adjusted quickly to my new surroundings at Jackson Sanitarium. I recall vividly that my hospital room had two beds in it. I occupied one of the beds and another boy about my age occupied the other bed. We enjoyed fun times together, even though we both had to remain in bed at all times.

The worst part of the experience that I remember was a repulsive white drink that appeared to be heavy cream from milk, but it didn't taste like milk. The nurse would practically force the drink down my throat and tell me that it was milk and good for me and that I must drink it. Often, I would throw it up, and she would feed it right back

---

[2] More information about LaRabida, a leading healthcare institution for children, is available at www.larabida.org.

to me. I had no choice in the matter. Now I realize that an awful tasting medicine was most likely put into the milk. My mother told me that I was being given cream because I was underweight. I never thought I was underweight.

For two or three years after I left the sanitarium, my mother continued to take me to see my heart specialist in Chicago, by train after we moved to Kenosha. I wish I could remember the Doctor's name. I do remember the dark room where he would examine my chest with a fluoroscope as I lay on a table. I was always fearful about what he would say to my mother and her close friend who accompanied us to the examinations. I recall the doctor's comments such as, "see, it's smaller" or, on another visit, "it's a little larger." I didn't know then, but I think now the doctor was referring to the size of myheart.

About fifty-five years later, I decided to visit the sanitarium to check my records. I was full of joy because they searched the archives and still had my records. They showed that I was there as a safeguard for suspicion of rheumatic fever.

I am fortunate that I did not have a serious heart problem. I recall clearly that I was often warned not to run and play. My mother would ask the doctor to repeat these warnings to me, because she told him I didn't listen to her. I didn't follow the doctor's instructions either. I liked to run and play with the other kids too much for that. I especially liked to play "Kick the Can," a form of soccer using a tin can, and I loved to play tag as well.

Chapter 3: Kenosha - Our New Home Town

Kenosha looked like a new town compared with the South Side of Chicago. Although I had been sad to leave my school friends in Chicago, I was thrilled to be there in our new house and next to my uncle, aunt, and cousins. I was eight years old; Emil was six and Vince was three.

My parents had worked hard scrimping and saving to be able to build their own house in Kenosha, an attractive brick home on the northwest corner of Twenty-Second Avenue and Fiftieth Street.

Our new house was located next door to my mother's older brother, Sam Chiappetta, his wife, Rafael, and their six daughters. We occupied the east corner of this relatively short block, and they occupied the west corner. The front of our house on Twenty-Second Avenue faced east, directly across the street from Ritacca's filling station. Three brothers owned the attractive station. It was a popular place. On the corner south of our corner, Mr. Spinelli owned Spinelli's Grocery Store. Corner neighborhood stores were everywhere. Supermarkets as we know them today didn't exist then. There was an empty lot kitty corner from us. The Aiello family lived next to the empty lot. Our address was 4922-22nd Avenue, Kenosha, Wisconsin. There were no ZIP codes until many years later.

We lived at a perfect location. Our every need was a short walk away. We lived only two blocks from Bain School, our grammar school, which had a large playground area and a softball/baseball diamond surrounded by a wire fence.

The Italian American (IA) Society building was across the street from Bain. My father and my uncle enjoyed playing cards at the IA. It was a popular place for weddings and other events.

We lived only three blocks from Holy Rosary Church. St. Anthony Church was only a block away, but we attended Holy Rosary. In addition to Spinelli's Grocery Store directly across the street from our house, Pierangeli's grocery was within two blocks.

I loved Bain School very much. It beat being in the confines of a hospital by far. I also enjoyed my new friends and loved playing tag, even if I wasn't supposed to play. I remember Dwight Busacca, who was really good at playing tag, weaving, in and out without getting touched. Then there was Eligio Pierangeli, whose father owned and operated the grocery store. I thought to myself, this is mighty good! I have a friend whose family owns a grocery store! I began to admire people who owned their own businesses.

Early School Days

I made many good friends at Bain and later at Washington Junior High School. In third grade or fourth grade, I had a crush on a girl in my class. I can't remember her name or what she looked like, but I remember I decided to tell my mother I wanted to get married. I don't recall what she replied. She probably said in Italian, "Are you crazy? You should pay attention to school!" Maybe I thought of marriage because I enjoyed the delicious candy and desserts I ate at wedding receptions our family attended at the Italian American Hall.

When I was nine, I transferred from Bain to the Orthopedic School for the Disabled in Kenosha. The school attended to the needs of children with all kinds of physical disabilities. I was there for about three months for continued supervision of my heart condition, and then I returned to Bain. I was still seeing my heart doctor in Chicago.

In those days, if a child received discipline from a teacher, it was not a good idea to complain about it at home. When I was in the fifth or sixth grade, I complained to my mother that a teacher had hit me on one of my hands with a ruler. "Show me where she hit you," she said.

I turned my hand and showed my palm.

She said sympathetically, "Let me see. Did she hit you here?" as she pointed to my palm.

I answered, "Yes, Ma."

The next moment, I felt and heard "Pow!" as she hit me across the side of my head with the back of her hand and said, "That's for me. You listen to your teacher! Do you hear?" That was the last time I ever complained to my mother about a teacher.

About this time, I began to show an interest in girls. My friend Carl Chiappetti (no relation) and I were both altar boys at Holy Rosary and were in the same classroom at Bain. Patricia Miller also was in our classroom and neighborhood. Carl and I both decided we should walk the two or three blocks to Patricia's house to see her. We had no idea what to do once we got there. Maybe we thought she would be outside and we could say "Hi!" But she wasn't, and we didn't knock on the door. We chickened out and left. I wish I could recall if I ever got up the nerve to talk to her.

My brother Emil and I loved to play baseball and practiced every chance we could get. We practiced often at Bain School's playground or an open field nearby after school. We would hit twenty or thirty fly balls to each other.

Colon Cancer Strikes Dad

My father was diagnosed with colon cancer in November 1934 when I was ten. He became an inpatient at St. Catherine's Hospital in Kenosha. Later he entered University Hospital in Madison, Wisconsin, for advanced care. He would be in the hospital for some time, back home, and then back in the hospital. His illness was very hard on my mother.

During times when Dad was home, he slept on the floor in our front room away from the bedrooms to quiet his outbursts of pain. He suffered tremendously. I recall his agony as though it were yesterday. My brother Emil also remembered our father's suffering. He and I both worried about cancer our entire lives, especially Emil. If my father was receiving pain medication, it wasn't doing any good. He was in such excruciating pain that he would scream out. I remember my mother telling me that he described the pain as a knife being struck into the back of his body. His colostomy did not help him.

My brothers and I did not live at home during the last months of his life, because my mother was attending to my father's illness at the hospital and staying with him frequently. I recall a time when she brought me with her to Madison for one of her visits to University Hospital. I was not allowed to visit my father. I remember the day we ate our lunch on a nearby park bench and enjoyed a rare treat, a small, yet delicious, piece of chocolate cake.

Near the end, my Mom found it emotionally and physically difficult to take care of us. Fortunately, our neighbors gave us the help and care we needed. My brother Emil and I stayed first with the Aiello family, who lived kitty corner from us. They had nine children: Jessie, Paul, Archangela, Jim, Victor, Elmer, Yolanda, Julio, and Frank. We slept there and ate all of our meals there. After we stayed with the Aiellos, we stayed with the Gallo family, who lived across the street from the Aiellos. We stayed with the Aiellos and Gallos because they had boys in the family. Grandma Newhaus, in Chicago, cared for my brother Vince. She was not a natural grandmother of ours, but we all called her Grandma. She was in her early eighties and was loved by all.

My father passed away during the night of February 26, 1937. University Hospital had sent him home the day before. I was twelve years old, my brother Emil was ten, and Vince was seven.

I recall that when I entered the kitchen the day Dad died, he was sitting on a chair, very thin and pale. We each shook his hand. I think he was too weak to hug us, but he did hug little Vince. That night at the Gallo's house, I had a sad dream that I remember to this day; I dreamt that my father had passed away. In the morning, Mrs. Gallo told me that my father had died during the night. I've never dreamed such a sad dream about anyone again.

Dad's body was laid out and available for viewing in a casket in our family room because we could not afford the services of a funeral home. Over two hundred friends and relatives came to pay their respects. I sat there for most of the two or three sad days while my father's body was shown.

Italians, especially women, express their deepest emotion when a loved one dies. The moment a close female friend or relative entered the room where my father's body lay, she would start crying out with incantations of sorrow and sadness for the death of a loved person. My mother would do likewise. Then they would embrace each other expressing their sorrow.

Dad was buried at St. George Cemetery overlooking Lake Michigan in Kenosha. The funeral director was Joseph Marinelli. In those times, the casket was lowered during the burial, witnessed by friends and relatives. The closed casket would be placed on a frame over the hole. People would surround the empty grave and prayers would be said. After prayers, the casket would be lowered into the hole. I vividly recall my mother standing at the head of the empty grave, and, in her utmost grief, moving forward to jump into the grave as the casket was being lowered. Fortunately, two strong friends, one on each arm, held her back.

I was very sad to see my father pass away. Many people told me he was a wonderful father and a hard worker. Prior to his cancer, he was a fireman at Nash (later American Motors, then Chrysler Motors); he shoveled coal into the hot furnaces all day long to support us.

As we look back on the days of my father's suffering and my mother's regular visits to the hospital, my brothers and I are deeply grateful to the Aiello and Gallo families for the help and loving care they gave to Emil and me, and for Grandma Newhaus' love and care of my little brother Vince.

During my father's illness and after his death, our church helped my family by providing Emil and me with clothing. I am forever grateful to the parishioners of Holy Rosary Church for their help.

Chapter 4: Making Five Cents an Hour

In the early years of the Great Depression, my mother, my brother Emil, and I worked on a farm during the summer to earn whatever we could. Dad was dead, and we had no other income. Our earnings were used for food and clothing. We worked for weeks, ten hours a day, six days a week, under the sun.

My brother and I, ages thirteen and eleven, were paid only five cents per hour. My mother received fifteen cents per hour. How much would these earnings be today? Using the Consumer Price Index, my wages today would be a paltry sixty-eight cents per hour, and my mom's wages would be a measly $2.03 per hour. But we were broke. We worked for whatever we could earn, or we didn't have a penny in our pockets.

We picked weeds between rows of onions on the Dinge, Sorenson, and Thompson farms near Kenosha. At 6:30 each morning, an open-panel truck would pick up twenty or twenty-five of us at a time. Two, three, or four members of each family would be picked up, brought out to the fields, and then brought home at the end of each day. Our neighbors the Aiellos, members of my friend Carl Chiappetti's family, my friend Al Bartolini who worked alone, my mother, Emil, and others rode in the truck. My brother Vince was too young to work on the farm at first, but he did so in later years of the Depression.

Large families like Carl's had more mouths to feed, but also more hands to share the work. Carl's family members came in bunches of ten. Carl's father and mother had ten children, Carl's grandfather and grandmother had had ten children, and Carl himself would eventually have ten too!

Everyone knew Carl's dad was a plumber. He walked to and from his jobs with his tools and a pipe cutter or bender on his shoulder. He was fortunate to know a trade at a time when unemployment was at the highest point ever in our country's history.

Even if someone in a family had a job, everyone else in that family needed to earn whatever money they could. Our work in the field started at 7:00 a.m. and ended at 5:30 p.m., with a half hour off for lunch. I don't recall that we had midmorning or mid-afternoon breaks.

During these hours, we crawled on our hands and knees in the dirt, wearing gloves, to pick weeds out by their roots between hundreds of rows of small onions referred to as onion sets. We rarely ever skipped work except for rainy days. As the day wore on, the summer sun would beat on our bodies, resulting in sweat, suntanned faces, and dirty bodies, especially on windy days.

We brought our lunches. We drank cool water from one or two large, clean galvanized garbage cans. We all shared the cans' dippers. Some days, the heat was almost unbearable. On those days, the water in the cans became warm in a short time, but we drank it anyway. We were not provided with any other comforts.

If it didn't rain, the ground became harder, making it difficult to pull the weeds with their roots attached. Parents brought cushions to use while kneeling and moving down the rows. At times, we would stand up and bend over to pick weeds rather than crawl just to change positions. And when the day was windy and the ground was dry, dust would swirl around us and blacken our cheap outer garments and the exposed parts of our bodies.

Then, several weeks later when the onions were ripe for picking, we would pick the sets, screen the dirt out, and dump the onions into a bushel basket. Each family group or worker would have a box about two feet square with a wire mesh to screen the dirt. Some of us would screen while others in the family continued to pull onions. We were not allowed to use tools other than our hands, to avoid injuring the onion sets. If the ground was damp or wet, we waited while onions rested in the screen box for the dirt to dry so we could more easily screen dirt away from the onions. If the ground was very dry, screening the dirt was easier and faster.

Each family worked together in their assigned row. We would receive a round brass chip for each bushel filled, and the chips were counted later for cash payment. The prettiest sight on earth was to look back and see our long row of bushels overfilled with onions that glistened golden-brown in the sun, waiting to get picked up by truck. This bounty of piled-up onions represented earnings in our pocket for our hard work. We received ten cents per bushel, so if my mother, brother, and I filled three bushels in an hour, an average rate, we shared thirty cents. That was slightly more than the total pay of twenty-five cents per hour the three of us earned for weeding onions. Some days we picked more than three or four bushels per hour, depending on the soil conditions. The Aiello family had three or four members picking. They were champions and picked more onions than any other family.

We were not allowed to take any onions home. I don't recall that we ever bought onions from the farmer, either. Frankly, onions look just as pretty and colorful today on vegetable counters as they did then. We hadn't developed distaste for onions just because we worked in the fields.

The money we earned was used for staple foods such as flour, eggs, and pasta. We needed to work hard on the farms to pay for food and clothing. And so we did.

Mom Becomes a U.S. Citizen

After my father died, my mother wanted to fulfill her dream to become a naturalized United States citizen. She didn't have to be able to read or write English to obtain a certificate of citizenship; however, she did need to be able to verbally answer questions about the U.S. Constitution; the Executive Branch; the Judicial Branch, especially the Supreme Court; and the Legislative Branch, including the Senate, the House of Representatives, and their responsibilities.

I helped her to memorize information about the president, including his name, duties, and terms of office; the names of the members of the Supreme Court; the number of Senate members for each state; and the election process for members of the House of Representatives. She passed her test and was awarded full status as a U.S. citizen at age forty-two. She signed her name on her certificate on June 22, 1937. She had practiced signing her name for weeks. Previously, she had signed her name with an "X."

My mother was indeed proud to become a U.S. citizen because now she would have the legal right to vote for the president and other government officials. She had not had voting rights in Italy. I don't know whether my father voted while he lived in Italy. To the best of my knowledge, he didn't apply for U.S. citizenship papers while living in Chicago or after moving to Kenosha. Both my parents loved America; they appreciated many of the freedoms enjoyed by U.S. citizens that we often take for granted. It bothers me when people don't vote, but then complain about lack of government support for their needs or about elected officials. We can't take our rights for granted or assume that elected officials know what we want.

Even though my mother didn't speak English very well at first, she learned to speak it quite well over a period of years. As a child, I felt a little embarrassed at times when I was with her and she did not "speaka the Engalish" very well. She did not attend school to learn how to read, write, or speak English. Her Italian lady friends, who raised fine families, didn't take the time to go to school. In the early years of my childhood, my brothers and I spoke Italian with my mother and father because they didn't understand English very well. Most fathers gradually learned to speak English at work in order to communicate with all Americans.

This was the norm for almost all of our Italian friends and relatives except my Uncle Sam and his wife and daughters. My uncle knew how to read and write English. He came to our country at age fourteen and learned quickly. Aunt Rafael spoke English fairly well but didn't read or write it. Initially, most families predominantly spoke Italian at home. As children grew older and spoke English full time at school with their friends and at home with their brothers and sisters, they exerted a strong influence on their parents to speak English. As time went on, many of my friends and I forgot how to speak Italian.

In time, as families moved away from Italian neighborhoods, or non-Italians moved into the neighborhood, it became imperative for the parents to speak better English to communicate with their neighbors, store clerks, nurses, physicians, and others. I recall my mother asking me what certain English words meant. Since my two brothers and I now spoke English at home almost all the time, my mother began to learn how to speak English from us.

She liked to listen to popular radio programs, as we all did, such as *Major Bowles Amateur Hour, Fibber McGee and Molly*, Bob Hope, and others. She especially enjoyed *Amateur Hour*, listening to many amateurs who sang songs in hopes of making the big time. She didn't understand all the words, but began to catch on. She improved her English even more when black-and-white television was introduced. She loved to watch television, especially *I Love Lucy*, after my stepfather bought her a TV about 1952. She and her friend would discuss how much they enjoyed Lucy's program. She especially enjoyed comedy shows.

It was easy to identify an Italian accent. Those from the old country would incorporate parts of their Italian words with English verbs. It was common to add vowels to English words or phrases, such as "Gooda luck to you," "Goda bless you," "I no speaka the Engalish," "Whatta ya name?" and "Is disa you house?"

As I entered my teenage years, I became very proud of my mother, even if she didn't speak good English. I knew she possessed an immense amount of courage and had suffered so much—the deaths of my father and Serafino, her own heart troubles, the way she worked washing clothes by hand for roomers, and her worries about supporting us. She and my father exemplified the spirit of hard work and sacrifice to overcome the difficult trials of illnesses, the deaths of loved ones, and poverty. I loved and respected them both to the highest degree.

Uncle Sam's Family

Although Uncle Sam Chiappetta was strict with his six lovely daughters, they all loved him and respected him. He established rules for my cousins, as one of them, Eleanora, explained:

> We were not allowed to have dates with young men until we reached age twenty-one. And we were not allowed to invite them to our house. (The only exceptions were Lydia and Elaine, who dated at eighteen and nineteen.) However, we were allowed one exception. We could attend Saturday night dances at the Italian American Society's Hall because my father, who was president of the Italian American, would be there for every dance. Most of my sisters didn't like to dance anyway, but Lydia and I went together a few times. Another thing, too, we were allowed to go to a movie, but only with one or two of our sisters, no one else.
>
> Until we reached age twenty-one, we could not keep what we earned at work. My dad asked for our entire paycheck but would allow us to keep a dollar and fifty cents per week for spending money. At age eighteen or nineteen, I argued with my dad over this matter, so I could purchase a Lady Hamilton watch. I wanted this watch very much. He allowed me to do so. I have this watch to this day.

I told her, "There's no doubt your dad was strict, but you all loved him very much. That's what I remember."

Eleanora replied:

> It's true, we did. We loved him and respected him. I remember one day, that one of our apple trees with its branches that hung over the sidewalk, was ready to be picked. My dad asked me to climb up this tree, as we usually did with all trees to pick apples. I

went up the tree with a ladder rather than shake the tree and bruise the apples. While up in the tree, I became suddenly sick. I couldn't make it down, and sat on the branch. My dad came up to get me and carried me down like a little lamb in his arms. He was pensive and looked so worried. My father and Mom didn't ever have a car or drive. My dad called our doctor, who came to the house. He rushed me to the hospital. I had suffered an appendicitis attack. I was operated on immediately to remove my appendix and all turned out well. You could see my dad was a loving father with utmost care and concern.

My uncle did allow my cousins the freedom to pursue their goals after they graduated from Kenosha High School or vocational school. Except for Eleanora, all the girls had their first job in the office at Coopers Company. Each of them was readily hired as a sister of Mary, who was the first to work there. Eleanora's first job was in the office for the Kenosha Youth Foundation. After they turned twenty-one, Mary and Eletta obtained positions in Washington, D.C. Mary worked for the General Services Administration, and Eletta worked at a bank. After a year or so, they returned to Kenosha. Except for Eletta, who worked in Illinois, and Eleanora, who worked in Milwaukee, my cousins remained in Kenosha, working primarily in banks.

We shared good times with my Uncle Sam, Aunt Rafael, and our cousins. My cousins loved my two brothers and me to death. When we were small boys, they would hug us, tell us children's stories, praise Emil and me for our altar boy services at Holy Rosary Church, and watch parades with us. My aunt and uncle also loved us. Eleanora told me, "He loved you three boys. He was so proud of you because you were boys and he didn't have any boys in his household. That is why, because you were old enough, he brought you, Sam, to the bike races at Washington Park."

We especially had fun when we shared major holidays, usually at their house because they had a larger home with a lower level used for cooking sumptuous meals. The lower level was also where they made ice cream. They would give us all the ice cream cones we wanted within reason, which was a real treat because we rarely could afford to buy ice cream. Emil and I were not monsters, but maybe we could have been classed as little devils at ages seven and nine. We did our share of taking cookies out of the cookie jar and did not always comply with warnings given to us regarding our behavior. My brother Vince was too little at the time to get in much trouble.

On one Easter Sunday while Emil and I were playing alone in the lower level, we discovered a covered blue enamel pan that contained a dozen hard-boiled, shelled eggs. They looked so very appetizing in their gleaming white coats. We couldn't resist the temptation. We sat down on the floor, made ourselves at home, and ate almost every egg. Emil ate the yellows, and I ate the whites. I didn't like the yellows. When my mother and aunt entered the lower level and saw we had eaten almost all of the eggs, we were scolded. In those days, parents, aunts, and uncles didn't hold back because they worried about a negative influence or unwanted psychological influence on their children. My mother confronted Emil and me, and said in Italian, "Umile! Sammie! You should be ashamed of yourselves. Why did you do that? What's the matter with you? You embarrass me. You act like I don't feed you! I hope you don't get sick! Now, you be good boys for the rest of the day, or we will go home! Do you understand?"

Emil and I knew she was really mad at us and both said, "Yes, Ma."

My aunt, a soft-spoken woman, advised us, "If you want something, ask your aunt. Don't take anything without permission. OK?"

We both answered, "OK."

My uncle was not inside the house while we were reprimanded. Our cousins also saw what we did, but didn't say anything. Whenever we boys did anything mischievous and were reprimanded by Mom or my uncle, our cousins never spoke about the matter. They remained quiet. My aunt's personality was normally quiet. When my uncle spoke, as head of the family, no one ever interrupted his discourse or offered opinions. In families from southern Italy, a father was the head of the family.

While my father was ill, Uncle Sam helped my mother care for us. She relied on his discipline when we did something wrong. With his stern voice and his spankings, he instilled fear into his warnings. My mother would say to Emil and me, "If you don't behave and listen to me, I will tell Uncle Sam!" Guess what? We listened! There is no way Emil or I wanted to be spanked by him. My mother knew that his spankings hurt and hers did not. I remember a couple of spankings I received from him. When he spanked me, my rear would really smart from the hit of his palm. I don't recall the reasons Emil or I were spanked.

In one of my recent conversations with Eleanora, I asked, "Why did my friends and others, including my brother and I, fear your father?"

She replied, "Uh, are you kidding? All he had to do was look at you! And the tone of his voice and his face showed authority too. When he would yell at the neighbor kids, he really didn't want them around to be sure they wouldn't climb up a tree and hurt themselves or to break branches. He worried about it. As a Kenosha County deputy sheriff, he was available to help control riots and lawbreakers from doing damage, and I think he thought he was a Gary Cooper when he wore his gun and badge."

Overall, I think we were good boys, just somewhat mischievous. Once when Emil and I were playing catch in our backyard, I threw the baseball over his head by mistake. It smashed right into my uncle's window across the alley and broke it into pieces. I thought for sure I would get it. But my uncle didn't spank me this time. I'm sure I looked scared. Maybe he saw so much fear, guilt, and sorrow in my face that he didn't have the heart to scold me or spank me. Instead, he said, "You broke the window, and I will not ask your mother to pay for it. I will fix it. But you should play with your baseball in your front yard and not here in your backyard. It's too close to my windows. There is more room in your front yard."

My aunt and uncle had about twenty apple trees in their side yard and backyard. This mini-orchard was located on the corner of Fiftieth Street and Twenty-third Avenue. A two-foot hedge surrounded the yard. My brother Emil and I enjoyed jumping over the hedge, picking up a couple of apples, and then jumping back over the hedge again on to the sidewalk. We thought this was a lot of fun! One day our uncle caught us in the act. He pulled us aside and scolded us. Then, he pleaded with us to stop taking his apples, saying that all we had to do was ask him, and he would give us apples.

"Sammie, you're the oldest," he said. "You want to set a good example for your little brother Emil! You should not jump over the bushes. Why do you want to steal my apples? You will damage my bushes and my yard! I will give them to you. Just come and ask me. I'm not going to bite you. Do you understand what I mean?"

Emil and I answered, "Yes, Uncle Sam. We won't do it any more."

We obeyed my uncle after his stern warning, but secretly we thought it had been more fun to jump over the bushes and take a few apples lying on the ground. My uncle would yell at my good friend Al Bartolini, who lived next door to him, when Al would stand on the public sidewalk next to the apple orchard and jump up to pick apples off the tree branches that hung out over the sidewalk. A couple of times, my uncle ran in his yard toward Al, exclaiming, "Don't do that! Get out of here! If you don't leave right now, I will get you!"

Al told me, "I didn't wait. I ran away as fast as I could."

Just recently, Al and I reminded each other how my uncle, bless his soul, offered to give us apples if we would simply ask for them.

There's no doubt that my uncle knew how to instill fear. When he was dressed as a deputy sheriff, kids thought he was a policeman, adding to their fear of his authority. Still, my uncle was respected highly as a charter member and one of the early presidents of the Italian American Society in Kenosha.

"Can I Have an Extra Orange, Please?"

A large percentage of Kenosha's population was on relief during the Great Depression. Help for the poor was not administered as a welfare program as it is today. Instead, I, like many others, would walk to downtown's relief headquarters according to schedule. I pulled my little red wagon, my best possession, behind me to pick up food. I would be given a bag or two of bread flour, breakfast cereals, a limited supply of fruits, perhaps pasta, and other foods I cannot recall.

I do remember asking for an extra fruit sometimes such as an apple or an orange. I would ask the man in charge, "Mr. Dicese, can I have an extra orange, please?"

I remember when he said, "Beat it, kid. I don't give any extras."

I didn't appreciate his response but I thought, "At least I tried. It's better than getting no food."

My walk to the relief center was about a mile each way. I always showed up for my time and date so our family would have food. I used my little red wagon not only to pick up groceries for our family, but also to deliver newspapers to earn extra income. The Depression era was tough for almost everyone in our town. We needed the food badly.

I'm glad, at this stage of my life, that I can give something back. This past Thanksgiving, I purchased one hundred meals for the poor and needy sponsored by our Milwaukee Rescue Mission. I've also applied to volunteer to deliver Meals on Wheels to the sick and elderly in our community. For many years, the companies I owned provided healthcare services to the sick and elderly.

We received food supplies at the relief center, but we received our clothing from a social worker, Miss Graham, at our home. She would visit our home on predetermined dates. My mother always reminded us when Miss Graham was scheduled to visit. Mom did not want us to miss an appointment. Miss Graham would bring us clothes, mainly blue overalls and shirts. These types of garment were cheap and used by hard-working farmers in their fields and by people who could not afford to buy clothes. Dress pants, when we got them, were usually too big around the waist. I wore pants that two of me could fit into. Sometimes, the items received didn't fit too badly. Sometimes, we received decent or nice-looking clothes from the Holy Rosary Church.

Today, I wince when I'm at a department store and see counters full of what we called overalls that are the same color as popular jeans. It reminds me of what the poor wore in the Depression years because we could not afford decent clothing. I once bought a pair of jeans to be in style. I wore them once and couldn't do it again. I have too many memories of being without the necessities of life or having very little to get by on.

I am fortunate to have close friends from those days who are still alive—Carl Chiappetti, Al Bartolini, and Frankie Santapaulo. We enjoy talking about those times, sixty-five to seventy years ago.

Our Greatest Blessing: Holy Rosary Church

When I was nine, I asked a priest at Holy Rosary if I could become an altar boy and serve mass. He approved, but said first I needed to learn Latin by attending instructions given by a priest at Mount Carmel, located across the street from Columbus Park. Our mass was conducted in Latin, and the altar boys had to answer prayers out loud in Latin during mass. I kept all my meeting dates with Father, and properly drilled and rehearsed my lines. When he felt I was ready, I became an altar boy at Holy Rosary, and served until I was fourteen, when we moved away to the west side of Kenosha. Emil followed in my footsteps and became an altar boy a year or two after I did. Uncle Sam's daughters praised us for becoming altar boys. None of them held such a position in the church because girls did not serve mass in those days.

The church became a central theme of my life's beliefs and those of my friends. We also played basketball at the church court and baseball in the field next door. Father Hartman loved baseball, and Father Oswald loved basketball. We enjoyed our church associations with all our hearts.

I made many good friends at Holy Rosary. We served mass regularly on Sundays and weekdays. I enjoyed attending catechism classes too. Every so often, we were treated to a sumptuous banquet in the basement where we enjoyed a good number of courses. The treatment we received from Father Hartman and Father Oswald was terrific and helped us to love and enjoy our association with one another, our religion, and the church and its activities.

Father Hartman encouraged us eleven- to fourteen-year-olds to play baseball. We played fast pitch softball. We had a good ball club. Besides me, Carl Chiappetti, Frankie Santapaulo, Gabriel (Gabe) Savaglio, Louis (LuLu) Gianelli, Tony Montuano, and others played on our team. I always liked Frankie's hitting because he could hit to right field, center field, or left field, and get hits. He was probably a .330 hitter. Carl was a good player too, and had his share of hits. I played third base and pitcher. I enjoyed pitching. I'd guess my batting average was about .275.

Father Hartman was an intense and nervous baseball coach. He inspired us to play our best. I noticed that on a couple of occasions during a game, he would have his hands behind his back, holding his cupped fingers of each hand grasped together, and rubbing the fingers together back and forth, in an intense fashion. He wanted us to win! I have always remembered Father Hartman's sincere and unselfish interests in our baseball activities.

Gabe was a darn good catcher. He would crouch behind the plate with his large glove. I loved to pitch to him. He took the game very seriously. I can still visualize how, as a kid of twelve or so, he would crouch and not flinch a bit when catching the ball on a batter's missed swing. He would talk to me at times, take his mask off, and I could see sweat rolling down the sides of his face. I would think to myself, Gabe is serious about playing and winning. He's a hard player. I need to pitch that ball in there for strikes! This is baseball! We are men playing this game!

Carl was a smart player with natural baseball talent. He could think fast and show his skills. We didn't keep batting average records. I'm guessing his batting average was .300.

The biggest game we ever had was in a tournament game in Racine, Wisconsin, about ten miles away from our church. We were excited and ready to play ball. Our opponents were at bat. We had the field. It was a close game. The bases were loaded. LuLu was pitching. Father Hartman was tense and excited. LuLu was getting ready to deliver his next pitch. Father Hartman yelled so everyone could hear. "Come on, LuLu! Burn it in there!"

LuLu threw his next pitch. The ball traveled higher and higher and sailed over the top of the back-up screen behind home plate. We lost the game.

Today, when Carl, Frank, and I see each other, we discuss our memories of this game and reminisce about Father Hartman's command to LuLu, "Come on, LuLu! Burn it in there!"

Carl was also smart as a basketball player; he seemed to catch on quicker and develop basketball moves faster than the other players on our team. Al Bartolini, another one of my best friends, was a very good basketball player. He showed natural talent in passing the ball and shooting baskets. Carl thinks Al was a better player.

We would choose team members for each side before each game. Father Oswald, our coach, also played on one of the teams. He enjoyed playing basketball just as we did. He played to win. He would run up and down the basketball court along with us. During these times, priests always wore their long black cassocks inside and outside the church and in public. They did not wear street pants and a shirt or street clothes except inside the rectory.

As Father Oswald would run up and down the court, the swishing sound of his cassock could be easily heard. We could hear swish, swish, and more swish. Fortunately, he was a fast runner. He undoubtedly would have been quicker than any of us, if he didn't have to wear his cassock.

I loved to play basketball and my mother knew it. She would not allow me to go play until I had cleaned the house, including dusting in the corners. At such times, I wished we had at least a sister or two.

As an altar boy at Holy Rosary, I served mass every Sunday, and often during weekdays and on holidays. The most difficult to serve was Christmas Eve mass; it was hard to stay awake. The mass would start at midnight and end at 1:30. This special mass was a high mass. I almost fell asleep a few times. One of the altar boys, Elmer Aiello, who was called Umps, fell asleep, fell over, and hit his chin on the marble steps. That woke him up! Fortunately, he didn't get injured.

Emil, the other altar boys, and I had fun. We put on our altar boy cassocks in the back of the church, behind the altar. The pull rope for the church bell was next to where we dressed. We took turns pulling down on that long rope, ringing the large tower bell so it would be heard within an area surrounding the church, approximately one to two square blocks. If a priest was not nearby, one of us would jump up off the ground to grab the rope as high as possible, pull it down and hang on to the rope for our free ride back up again until the rope reached near the top to ring the bell on its other interior side. It was fun! When more than one altar boy was present, there would be slight disagreements about whose turn it was to toll the bell.

I will always be thankful for the wonderful memories I made and lessons I learned through my association with Holy Rosary Church. Even when my friends, my brothers, and I were "just having fun," we were strengthening our faith and our characters, building strong foundations for the men we would become.

Chapter 5: Middle School Memories

I entered seventh grade at Washington Junior High School in September 1937. Today, it is called Washington Middle School. I could feel the excitement of this transition to a new school to join with older kids. Some of the ninth graders were taller and larger than I expected. This was no longer elementary school, but a stepping-stone to high school. There were many more kids in the middle school than the elementary school.

I thought, "Here I am a little kid, now getting together with big kids." I knew that I would enjoy the thrill of scholastic challenges. Although I loved to play and engage in sporting activities, I felt I wasn't a kid anymore. Physically, I didn't have the weight or the physical strength to complete. I was beginning to find that out when we played football at Oat's Field next to Holy Rosary Church. When I blocked or tackled a bigger kid, who had fifty or more pounds on me, I felt it. All my bones rattled. I think I had the ability and the smarts, but not the size.

School kids and their parents respected their teachers. My friends and I and the other kids at our school wanted to have good grades, and most of the kids applied themselves to their best ability. Except for rare cases, children did not smoke, drink, take drugs, or have sex. Religion played an important part in the students' lives, whether we were Catholic, Protestant, Evangelist, or Lutheran. We had good examples for governing our behavior. We had radio, with soft types of music, or radio programs, and baseball games, but no television, computers, or cell phones.

During this time, I also attended confirmation classes at Holy Rosary. Confirmation was an important part of our lives, signifying we would be entering the mature stages of our lives as devout Catholics. My sponsor for confirmation, often also called godfather by Italian folks, was a long-time friend of my parents, Peter Pulice from Chicago. He stood by me on the day I was confirmed by the archbishop. I still can recall very clearly kneeling at the altar and receiving his blessings of confirmation and his sign of the cross on my forehead.

A Rough Time for Emil

In 1938, Emil lost the vision in his left eye. He was at Oat's Field, and one of the girls from our neighborhood was also there. She had a tendency to be a tomboy. Emil was eating a bunch of grapes as he walked. He heard her yell, "Emil! Give me some of your grapes." Emil turned around and said no. She was carrying a BB rifle.

She yelled again, "If you don't give me any grapes, I will shoot you!" Emil turned his head to see if she was going to shoot at him. She pulled the trigger, and a BB hit my brother's left eye. I recall how he cried from the pain. Despite medical care, he never regained his sight in that eye. Friends and relatives didn't sue each other then, and medical liability insurance was unknown.

Sometime later, my mother bought a used violin for Emil. She arranged with a music teacher to give Emil lessons for fifty cents a week. Emil practiced in our second-floor flat. Mom had borrowed money on a second mortgage to pay for these additional rooms and then rented out the larger first floor. Whenever Emil practiced, I would think to myself that he was an awful player. But then, I knew I was not a good judge of music or violin playing. One day, my mother was out shopping and happened to bump into Emil's teacher. My mother asked her, "By the way, how is Emil doing with his violin?"

The teacher replied, "With his lessons? Don't you know? I haven't seen Emil for weeks. I thought he quit. I thought you knew that, Mrs. Ruffalo."

When Mom got home, he really received a whale of a lecture. He had spent all of the money that was given to him for his lessons. Then I knew why he played so terribly. He didn't go to his lessons!

Sport and Movie Memories

I had always had an interest in sports. I began to take an interest in boxing and listened to the Joe Louis fights on the radio at my Uncle Sam's house in 1934 when I was ten. Louis was called the Brown Bomber. My uncle was a great fight fan and listened to all the championship bouts. Not all fights were broadcast in those years. In 1935, Louis defeated Primo Canera and Max Schmeling, who were top contenders. Louis began his career in 1934, and fought in the ring for many years.

A few years later, golf caught my attention. My brother and I began to learn and play golf at Washington Park's golf course. We liked to play, but we could only rarely afford the fifty-cent greens fee; and fifty cents was cheap considering better courses cost sixty cents to one dollar. In later years, we could afford it. Emil was a good golfer, but I'm sure he would have been even better if he had had vision in his left eye. Still, he never complained about it.

I also enjoyed listening to baseball games. Everyone in our town remembers Chicago Cub catcher Gabby Hartnett's home run September 28, 1938, in the last of the ninth inning with two outs and two strikes, to win the National League pennant for the Cubs. He was a great catcher, and the Cubs' manager. I was listening to the game, as were many others in Kenosha. The men across the street who owned and worked at Ritacca's filling station cheered so loud that I could hear them through the windows in our house. Most Kenosha baseball fans were Chicago Cub fans. We were only sixty miles from Chicago, and Milwaukee didn't have a major league baseball team until many years later. All of my friends in Chicago were very thrilled as well.

Even though I physically wasn't cut out to play football, I enjoyed watching the Kenosha Cardinals semiprofessional football games. Sometimes, if I had a nickel, I would place it in a hat when a hat was passed around to help players purchase their uniforms and other gear.

If and when we grew tired of sports, we could turn to the movies for added entertainment. We were now able to afford the dime admittance to watch a few movies. My first favorite movie star sweetheart was Alice Faye, who played in *Alexander's Ragtime Band* in 1938. I thought she was very beautiful. It was a light musical and love story. Tyrone Power, Kenosha's Don Ameche, Ethel Merman, and Jack Haley also starred in this film. *Alexander's Ragtime Band* was Don Ameche's first major movie.

Now, in 2005, Kenosha has provided another movie star, Mark Ruffalo, who is gaining in real popularity. To the best of my knowledge, I'm not related to Mark Ruffalo. He comes from a neighborhood in Kenosha that was very close to the neighborhood where I was brought up.

I would be remiss if I didn't name my favorite movie, an all-time classic, *Gone with the Wind* (1939). The movie was three and a half hours long with an intermission, of course. The main actors were Clark Gable, Vivien Leigh, Olivia de Havilland, and Leslie Howard.

Mother Remarries

In the three years following my dad's death, my mother had dated only a handful of times. Then, one day, my mother told me that a man she had recently met would be coming to our house so I could meet him. He looked to be a fine man and a friendly person. I was told to call him Tom. His full name was Thomas Rotunda. I learned he lived at Thirty-first and Sixtieth Street, a block away from Nash (later American Motors), where he was employed.

While Tom was visiting us, I noticed a new-looking black beauty four-door Buick parked in front of our house. I thought to myself, "Is that his car? Holy mackerel!" We didn't have friends or relatives who owned such a good-looking auto. It was indeed Tom Rotunda's car, a 1938 Buick. I will admit it was an impressive experience to see such a car parked on our curb.

He continued to court my mother. One day, my brothers and I were brought to his house at 3104 S. Sixtieth Street. It was also located on a corner and contained a nice-sized kitchen, a living room, a bedroom on the first floor, and two bedrooms upstairs. The kitchen had a large white refrigerator. The refrigerator door was opened and I was offered a glass of chocolate milk. Holy mackerel! I never ever had a glass of chocolate milk in my life! While the door was opened, I could see the refrigerator was full of food. This is a sight I was not used to. I did think that if we were at his house, he and my mother were serious about each other. I sensed that Tom would bring security and stability to our lives if they would get married.

On September 14, 1940, my mother and Thomas were married in Kenosha. We moved from 4922-22nd Avenue into our new house. My mother kept our previous house and rented out the upper flat. My brothers and I called our stepfather Dad. We respected him as a father. I was the oldest of the boys, and felt a deep appreciation for him because he took us in and provided for us. Until the day my stepfather died, I loved, respected, and honored him. To this day, when I visit my father and mother's graves at St. George Cemetery in Kenosha, at least twice each year, I also visit my stepfather's grave in the same cemetery. I also visit my uncle and aunt's graves nearby.

My stepfather had been married twice before. Both wives had died due to illness. He had seven children, all older than me, from those marriages. At this time, I was sixteen, Emil was fourteen, and Vince was ten. Thomas' children Tommy, seventeen, and daughter Rose, in her late thirties, lived with their dad for a while. Rose left first for her own place, and Tommy left a year later. Thomas' other children were Mary, Gloria, Frank, Tony, Orlando, and Armando.

Outsmarting the Upholsterer

Shortly, after we moved to our new home, I started a part-time job, getting up at 4:00 a.m. to deliver the *Milwaukee Sentinel* on weekdays. Paper were delivered to me at the North Shore train station each morning located near to my house. I would put them in my large canvas shoulder bag and walk my route during all seasons of the year. I also took another part-time job at a nearby upholstery shop. I still kept up good grades.

The upholstery shop owner hired me for fifty cents per hour to remove existing and worn material from couches and chairs so he could rebuild them. I would start with the back of a furniture piece most of the time and then remove the sides followed by the arm coverings. After the coverings were removed, I needed to remove the interior padding material from the seating cushions or the seating area, the back of the front area, the sides, and the arms. Taking a piece of furniture and removing all of its insides was no fun. Foam rubber was not a part of furniture in those days; cloth fabrics and inside stuffing were extremely dusty and difficult to remove around tacks and nails imbedded into the wood.

I worked about three to four hours a day after school to 7 or 8 p.m. and six to eight hours on Saturdays. I had asthma and was highly allergic to dust and wool. I would regularly sneeze and blow my nose a lot on the job and on the way home. The shop owner paid me each Friday the first couple of weeks. Then, he told me that he would pay me the next week. On that week, he said he would pay me for two weeks the next Friday. On the next Friday, he didn't pay me either, and said he would pay me for three weeks the next wek, so I quit.

My mother didn't like it that I wasn't paid. When she married Thomas Rotunda, my brothers and I kept our last name of Ruffalo. The upholsterer didn't recognize the name Rotunda when my mother called him to come over, give her an estimate to reupholster a chair, and pick it up if the price was right. My mom was sure to let me know when he would be over so I would be away. He came to pick up the chair as scheduled and my mother selected the fabric she wanted. When he finished the chair at his store, he delivered it to her. After he placed the chair down, he gave her the bill. At this point, she asked him if he remembered me working for him. He said, "Yes."

She said, "Sam is my son. He worked for you. You did not pay him. I'm going to pay you, but I'm going to deduct the amount that you owe to Sam for his work. I will give you the difference. If you don't accept this, I won't pay you at all." He accepted payment. I thought my mother was smart. Even though she could not read or write English, she was a smart lady.

A short time later, I got a better job. I became a counter clerk inside the North Shore Station and sold newspaper, cigarettes, candy, and miscellaneous items. Our best sellers by far were packs of cigarettes. I enjoyed waiting on these passengers and making friends with them. Most of them traveled from Kenosha to Chicago or Milwaukee every day.

My friend Al Bartolini lived next to my Uncle Sam and across the alley from my yard. Al and I worked together on Sundays for about a year delivering the *Chicago Tribune* to a large number of subscribers. We would go to the Henoch News Agency office near downtown, pick up our Sunday papers in a wagon, and deliver the newspaper to our customers. We split our profits 50-50. We have always laughed about how we kept track of whose turn it would be the next week to receive the left over penny if the 50-50 split was not even.

Chapter 6: Growing Up Fast

Our nation was unprepared for Japan's attack on Pearl Harbor on December 7, 1941. The life of every man, woman, and child would be affected.

The U.S. draft began on October 16, 1940, in response to Hitler's European conquests. All men between the ages of twenty-one and thirty-five had to register with their local draft boards for possible service. The draft eventually targeted men as young as eighteen.

Our school decided to make it mandatory for boys to take a cooking class so we would be prepared as a cook if drafted. Every one of us enjoyed the one-hour class and had fun cooking different meals, but we failed miserably in our cleanup duties. We were instructed to always clean up our work areas and put items back in their place ready for use by the next class, the girls in our school. We did a poor job of it, and they often complained.

My brother Emil quit high school in the tenth grade and didn't have cooking class. So of course, he became a cook in the U.S. Army. Of all people who should not be cooks, Emil was at the top of the list. One of his jobs was to boil and prepare chickens to serve to soldiers. After the war, and for the rest of his life, he wouldn't touch or look at a piece of chicken whether it was roasted, fried, boiled, or grilled.

Only a block away from our house were Pitts' Pool Parlor, owned by my good friend Al "Bud" Pitts' father, and Frank's Sweet Shop, owned by Robert Chiapetta's father (no relation to my mom's family). As long as sixty-five years later, Bob, Al and I and our wives have spent hours of fun in their kitchens and ours, many times making home-made pasta, pasta dishes, and Italian sauces for freezing. We share a bond of deep love for our families. Bob and Laura have children and grandchildren who love one another dearly, as do Evelyn and Al and their family members.

I learned to play pool in the early part of 1941 and enjoyed the game for many years thereafter. Bud Pitts was good to me and would allow me to play a free game every now and then, and didn't charge me when I ordered an ice cream bar. There were many young men from our area who played at Pitts' Pool Parlor. I recall some of the names but not as many as I wish—Frank Pitts, Bud's older brother;

Joe Pacetti, a good pool player; Husky Swanson; Norman Bell; Bob Flocker; and Tony "Oink" Milkus. The cost of one game between two players was only five cents in 1941 and 1942. The youngsters who came there were good people and did not lead troublesome lives. We played two games most of the time and very little billiards. Our favorite game was eight ball.

Bob Pitts, Al's younger brother, who to the best of my memory didn't play pool at the time due to his young age, became well known in Kenosha as a business leader and for his community service. His dedication to Kenosha is not surprising given his family's longstanding ties to the community.

Later in life, I bought a regulation-sized pool table with a one-piece slate bottom for my recreation room and kept this table for approximately forty years. I had a lot of fun playing pool with my children, relatives, and friends. The children also used it with their friends.

Tuning into Transmitters and Receivers

After moving to our new neighborhood on Thirty-first and Sixtieth Street, I became good friends with Waldo E. Bauer, who we called Wally. We both had a great interest in building radios, receivers, and small transmitters from scratch as a hobby. We spent a lot of time together experimenting and building equipment, including our first crystal set, a simple set for listening to radio station broadcasts. Then we advanced to building our own radio receivers and small transmitters. We didn't have much money to buy new parts from Radio Shack, so we would visit places that sold used parts. We prayed they would work when hooked up, and most of the time, they did. I also became friends with Wally's brother Bob, and Wally's two good friends John Robertson, and Caesar Banks.

We used parts such as resistors, condensers, little transformers, radio tubes, toggle switches, tube sockets, and many other items to build radios and transmitters. Radio tubes looked similar to a light bulb, but in a rectangular shape. A tube's prongs would be plugged into a female socket on a chassis where all parts were assembled before it was set inside an appropriate metal case. A chassis could be compared in a way to a computer motherboard. Radio tubes were called diodes, triodes, and pentodes. The inside of these tubes also contained elements called cathodes and plates used to receive modulated waves or signals and convert them into sound.

High School Memories

I enjoyed high school studies and received As and Bs. I completed my assignments and fared well in my tests. For some reason I had difficulty with social studies. Our school offered a class in Italian. The class was mostly made up of kids like me who already knew how to speak Italian. Mr. Magaro, an Italian himself, taught this class. Naturally, many students from Italian families passed with flying colors.

With very few exceptions, all the kids at Kenosha High, now called Mary D. Bradford High School, were good kids. Each had a unique personality. Boys were beginning to shape into manhood, and girls were beginning to shape into womanhood. We had many pretty girls in our school. I began to say hello and exchange a few words, and later, even carry on a conversation with them. I had a crush on a couple of girls during high school. I did not know how to dance so I didn't ever attend a prom. I wish I had. My buddies from the west side of Kenosha were pretty much the same.

I loved playing and watching sports and thoroughly enjoyed going to our high school basketball and football games. I didn't have the size or weight—five foot six and 135 pounds—to try out for any teams. Kenosha High had a fine basketball team and a very good football team. Our quarterback star and hero was Lester Salerno, who could pass the football sixty yards at a time. His favorite receiver was Angelo Calvarese, whom we called "Honk." Honk lived in Lester's neighborhood, and they practiced a lot together at Washington Junior High before getting to Kenosha High. They were outstanding players, and the best players on the team. They are very good friends to this day. I was lucky to have both of them in homeroom and a few classes in high school. We all loved them. Calvarese was the only receiver on our team who could catch Salerno's sixty-yard passes.

My longtime friend Carl Chiappetti, who lives near my house, and I have driven to Kenosha so we could visit with Calvarese and Salerno and others at McDonald's in Kenosha and visit some of the sights for old times sake. These old-timers meet there regularly for breakfast.

I love to go to our high school class reunions. Our sixty-fifth reunion is scheduled for 2008. I won't miss it if I can help it. I always leave with an exalted feeling, especially when I hear, "Sam, you look great! You haven't changed a bit. I could recognize you anywhere." That compliment takes about twenty years off my life!

One of my favorite teachers in high school was Miss Loew, who taught history. She was perhaps the oldest teacher in our school, and we used to kid around she was old enough to be a part of our history studies.

My favorite male teacher was Mr. Stoker. He came to one of our class reunions when he was in his eighties. He taught hygiene; only boys were allowed to attend this class because it was intended to be about the birds and the bees, meaning a hint about sex matters. I don't recall any discussions in our classroom about sex or about sexual relations between men and women. The words "sex" and "sexy" were not used. I do recall, however, one of Mr. Stoker's precepts. He said, "The trouble with you guys is you don't know how to compliment a lady. Don't say to her, 'You look pretty with your new dress.' Instead, tell her, 'My, you're pretty and sure make your new dress look beautiful.'" I remembered and used it. The girls loved it.

Any Job to Earn a Buck

Working As a junior and senior, I worked at any job I could find. One of these jobs was as a pinsetter at Gutormsen's bowling alley for a few months. In these times, machines were not used to sweep, pick up, and set pins. Pins were set up by hand. A pin boy would take care of two alleys at one time, jumping over the alley divider board that was about two feet high. While in the pit, the pin boy quickly picked up the pins and placed them into the rack and then pushed a lever down to set them on the alley. He then jumped over the sideboard to do the same things for the next alley, and then back again to the previous alley, all night long for four hours or so. If a pin boy wasn't in shape when he started, he certainly was after about a week of this kind of work.

I also shined shoes at Roselli's shoe shop in downtown Kenosha with my friend Al "Bud" Pitts on Saturdays for about a year. We each shined about fifty to seventy-five pairs of men's shoes during the day. A man would enter our shoeshine parlor, step up one step to a chair, and place his shoes on a raised foot pedal. We each would start the procedure, first with one shoe and then the other. Our first step would be to wash the first shoe with saddle soap using a brush, and then dry it. We then applied polish by hand with our fingers placed together to use the fingers and the inside of our hand as a pad. We then went on to the next shoe and did the same. Then it was time to go back to the first shoe and use the shine brush, held in one hand to quickly and thoroughly brush the shoe. Then we would grab a rectangular size cloth at each end, pull the cloth to be tight, and in fast motion slide it back and forth over the front and sides of the shoes.

Mr. Roselli was a large rotund man. His daughter came to the shop on Saturdays just to visit her father. She was always immaculately dressed with her high heels and stockings and wore lipstick and powder. John, the shoemaker, concentrated on his job except when the ladies walked into the shop. He never missed one walking in the door. He kept one eye on his repair work and the other on the ladies. I would say he was about thirty-five years of age at the time. He only repaired shoes. He did not converse or deal with the customers. He worked strictly behind the counter in the area that contained the motors, brushes, and tools.

Bud and I would work until 9:00 p.m., and then put our things away before going home. We would joke around and laugh about some of the funny things that happened during the day. I can recall one of Bud's favorite acts was to use shoe polish to form a mustache, then look in the mirror and start acting as if he were Clark Gable. We enjoyed our day's work and the tips we earned. Each of us would receive about seven or eight dollars in tips for our day's work.

I also worked as a rod man assisting the survey engineer for the construction of airplane engine test cells during the summer of 1942. The government had contracted to build airplane test cells adjoining the Nash automobile plant. Plans called for several test cells to be constructed immediately to test Pratt and Whitney engines before shipment. A test cell was built of cement and sound barrier blocks and had a height of eighty feet.

The construction company's general foreman came to our house in answer to an ad for our upstairs vacant apartment in June 1942. Due to the large contract for test cells, there was a shortage of flats and apartments. Our house was within six blocks of where the test cells would be built. My mother told him she would rent the apartment to him if he would give me a job. When I told him I was taking trigonometry in high school, and he asked me if I thought I could help the surveying engineer. I answered that I thought I could. He then asked, "Do you know what a rod man is?"

I took a chance and answered, "Yes." I was also thinking about what I would say if he asked me to explain what a rod man did.

Fortunately, he didn't ask me; he just told me to show up for the job in the morning and ask for the chief engineer. As soon as he left, I ran across the street to the corner drugstore and asked the pharmacist and the owner Mr. Lemiuex, "Ray, what does a rod man do on construction?" He explained how a rod man assists the surveyor and moves a pencil up and down the measuring stick to measure heights and depths needed to prepare foundation for construction of buildings, projects, and highways.

Because I thought I would be working with professional engineers, I believed I should go to work dressed up. I put on my green sport coat (the only sport coat I had owned up to that date), dress pants, a white shirt and a tie, and street shoes.

The next morning, I found the chief engineer, introduced myself, and explained the general foreman had asked me to meet with him. The chief engineer appeared to be in his mid fifties. He welcomed me and then informed me that workers don't dress up for construction work. I took off my coat and tie. A little later in the morning, I met the engineer, Andy, with whom I would be working. Andy was a great guy. He was a twenty-five-year-old engineering graduate from Purdue University. He took me under his wing and gave me detailed instructions. I was lucky it all turned out this way. I don't think anyone was fooled regarding the lack of my skills, but I began to learn from Andy, and worked close with him every day. Andy and I got along really well. We went to a movie together a couple of times.

I received forty dollars a week in wages. I was delighted to have my first real job that I liked, one that would pay me well, and wouldn't involve me working in a sweatshop. My morale was at an all-time high.

My surveying job lasted about six weeks. Andy had completed most of his tasks that needed my services as a rod man. By this time, the test cells were up. The foreman told me that my new job would be to wheel a wheelbarrow full of cement blocks from one cell to the next cell building so that the workmen could use them for completing construction of the cell. When I got to the top of the cell, I was never more scared in my life. First, these cell blocks were eighty feet high. I didn't like heights. Then I was told to haul the blocks in the wheelbarrow to the next cell over the boards that spanned the distance between two cells. I didn't like that the two boards consisted of two twelve-foot boards placed next to each other, giving me about a two-foot walkway from one cell to the next. I was terrified. I wasn't going to quit. I prayed. I looked over to the next cell, and there a fellow was hauling blocks from one cell to the other and walking a normal pace. His walkway was only two boards. I thought, "He's nuts!"

But I started my first trip between two cells. There was no way I would walk the way the fellow in the next cell did. I took it very slowly, one measured step after another to be sure I wouldn't step off the boards. My first wheelbarrow trip across to the next cell took forever. I noticed the fellow at the cells next to me would whistle while he walked at a normal pace. I was not going to quit. I kept at it. By the afternoon, I was a little better at it and had gained more confidence. The next day I was walking across the cells just like the fellow next to me. I was proud of myself that I had overcome my fear of heights. But in reality, I still think this was dangerous.

In the summer of 1943, I worked on the assembly line at the Nash Motors Company. I didn't have far to walk because I lived a block away. Nash management was understandably consumed with mass production and the production of more automobiles each day.

Years later, the Rambler became the most popular Nash model. I owned a red convertible Rambler in the '60s. The Rambler was the first compact car sold in the postwar era. It was the only convertible I ever owned, and I liked it. Nash and the Hudson Automobile Company merged in 1954 to form American Motors, and the Rambler remained the company's leading seller. In 1987, Chrysler Corporation acquired American Motors. I eventually got used to calling the plant the Chrysler plant when visiting friends and relatives in Kenosha.

I didn't ever think I would want to work at Nash. I remember vivid scenes of men inside the wire fence gates on the corner of Sixtieth Street and Thirtieth Avenue with their fingers on the fence looking out. If my friends and I ever had a goal in life, it was to stay out of that automobile factory.

Why? First, I wasn't thinking of studying and going on to college so that I could work at Nash, by far the major employer in Kenosha. Secondly, it was a sweatshop. My father began working there in 1932, as a fireman shoveling coal into furnaces. He was an unskilled laborer and worked fourteen hours per day. We moved to Kenosha from Chicago so he could work there and support us. His long white underwear didn't stay white very long due to the coal dust. They looked almost pure black when my mother would wash them.

My stepfather also worked at Nash and then American Motors for many years. He did not work in the foundry. My brother Emil worked at Nash, later American Motors, starting in the foundry. When I would feel his hands, I thought I had a piece of steel wool or hardened skin. Later, Emil served as a union steward. Unions became very powerful before and after the postwar era. Later he became a paint department foreman. He enjoyed his job but would get ulcers dealing with union and racial problems.

So what was I doing at the Nash plant in the summer of 1942? I planned only to work there during the summer months before returning to high school. Attending high school was my first priority.

My job on the assembly line entailed placing screws into the rubber matt at the base of the steering column to cover up the steel in the chassis. Automobile bodies with their frames were placed on a floor conveyor belt and moved along for workers to each perform their tasks. I used a drill and drill bit with a Phillips head tip to screw in about eight screws into the rubber and attach it to the floor at the base of the column. I would jump into the car with my drill and bit, crouch underneath the steering wheel and screw in the screws, jump out right away, and jump into the next car and repeat this action over and over again.

This job is OK for a young man who doesn't have back problems. I qualified. It was hard work for eight hours a day with a half-hour break for lunch and one fifteen-minute break in the morning and one in the afternoon. Today, automobile makers use robots for jobs.

They needed a worker in the tire department, so I was transferred there. I learned how to place a tire on a rim after inflating its inner rubber tube. The procedure was simple but required fast action to keep up with the demand. I would pick up a new tire, throw it onto the tire rotator machine, and hold and insert the tire iron to ensure that the tire would fit snugly inside the rim. The machine where the tire was placed kept turning automatically and continuously.

During the school year, I worked part time for my stepbrother Orlando. He owned a radio repair shop not far from our neighborhood. He made some repairs in the shop and others at his customers' homes. He would schedule his house appointments and then let me know when I should stay in the store and take care of his customers. He didn't pay me much, but then I didn't do much except stay in the store, to greet a customer, and obtain information to pass on to Orlando. When I wasn't busy with customers, I studied and prepared my school assignments. Orlando eventually moved out of the city to Colorado, I believe, to open up a radio shop there.

"It Isn't a Car?"

Shortly before I graduated from high school, my brother Vince and I were upstairs in our bedroom before turning in for the night. He said to me, "I know what you're getting for your graduation."

I said, "Is it really a nice present?"

He replied, "It's really nice. You are going to be surprised."

I asked, "I am? What am I getting?"

He answered, "I can't tell you. It's a nice surprise."

I was going to be age nineteen on June 18, and Vince was thirteen. I told him to tell me. He wouldn't. I asked him again, with a warning in my voice. I'm not sure he was frightened, but excitedly he said, "You're getting a nice gold watch for your graduation!"

In a disappointed voice I said, "What! A watch! I don't want a watch! It isn't a car?"

I had been hoping I would get a car for my graduation. I certainly wasn't thinking smart. First, we didn't have anywhere near the kind of money to expect that my parents would purchase a car for me, though I would have taken any old junker.

I continued: "I don't need a watch! What am I going to do with a watch?" I was disappointed. After a pause, I angrily said, "Go downstairs and bring me up the bottle of grappa." He hurried downstairs, returned, and handed me the bottle.

Anyone who has ever swallowed a shot of grappa knows it is a very strong liquor. It tastes stronger than 100 percent proof. I knew it was strong so I sipped my first whiskey glass of it. Then I took a second shot and drank it slowly. I was not used to drinking hard liquor. I was somewhat used to drinking wine we used for family holiday dinners and some beer.

Our bedroom upstairs had one bed for me and a double bed for Vince and Emil. Emil wasn't home. After drinking three or four shots lying in my bed, I began to mumble my words and talk foolishly. I talked aimlessly about my trip to Africa, even though I had never been anywhere other than Kenosha or Chicago, and described my escapades in Africa with Paulette Goddard, a popular movie star. I rambled on quite a bit, slurring my words. Vince was either confused or amused, having a ball listening to his older brother babble on aimlessly.

Across from our bedroom lived Peter Falcone and his new bride, Josephine. Everyone loved this couple. They were about to enter their apartment at the head of the stairs when they heard some commotion in the bedroom. Pete knocked and opened up the door to see what was going on. In my drunken condition, I asked him to come in. He and Josephine began laughing at me. Pete liked to drink once in a while, so I thought of an idea. Slurring my words, I asked, "Pete, you can have a drink if I can kiss Josie. Is that a deal?"

They were laughing very hard, and Pete answered, "OK with me." Josie kissed me. I didn't recall anything after she kissed me. I must have passed out right then.

The next morning, I felt very sick with a dizzying hangover I hadn't ever experienced before. Pete was sick enough that he didn't go to work. He obviously had more than the one drink I had offered him. While I was sitting in the kitchen feeling sick, my mother asked me if I remembered going to the bathroom during the night. I didn't. Our family only had one bathroom for our part of the house. It was located on the first floor next to my mothers and stepfather's bedroom. To get to the bathroom, one needed to walk through their bedroom. My brothers and I had learned to walk through the bedroom quietly so as to not awaken Mom and Dad.

She informed that I did come downstairs to go to the bathroom. She confirmed that during the night she heard some noises in the bathroom that woke her up. She found me lying in the bathtub. She woke me up and told me to go to bed where I belonged. She was starting to fall back to sleep when she started to wonder why I was lying in the bathtub. She walked upstairs to find out if I had returned to my bed. Reflection from our street corner lights shone through our shades and added some light to our bedroom.

As she opened the door, she saw liquid on the mattress, and immediately thought it was blood. She had no idea I had been drinking our liquor. She turned on the light. She was relieved to not see any blood but was puzzled until she smelled liquor. She noticed I had vomited. Mom cleaned it up. I was still so drunk I didn't feel or hear anything at all. I was so sick during the night I didn't know any of this had happened. I explained to my mother what had happened and why I drank our house liquor with Pete. I can tell you she didn't have any words of praise. Later that day, Pete and I began to feel better. Never again in my life did I drink to the point of unconsciousness. I learned a good lesson.

Fortunately, I had enough time to get rid of my headache before I celebrated my high school graduation. I attended our ceremonies at school with a full life ahead of me.

Chapter 7: Serving My Country in World War II

Shortly after graduating from high school and being of age, I received a letter from Uncle Sam to report for the draft. I reported for my examinations, but was rejected with a 4-F classification due to my heart trouble as a child. I also had asthma. I was extremely disappointed; I wanted to serve in the armed services and do my part as well.

Soon after my rejection, I learned about electronic courses available at Coyne Radio School in Chicago. I enrolled in September 1943 and moved into Chicago and rented a room. I remember my first class very well; Mr. Barlow asked, "What is electricity? Sam?"

I said, "I don't know."

He said, "You're right, Sam! No one knows." All students agreed he was one whale of a good instructor.

After completing my courses at Coyne the following April, I scheduled my examinations with the Federal Communications Commission (FCC) for a 2nd Class Telephone License and a 2nd Class Telegraph License. I passed both exams, and was therefore qualified to send and receive Morse code and to operate and repair receivers and long distance transmitters at high frequencies. In those days, receivers obtained short-range voice signals and transmitters were used to receive and send code over thousands of miles.

There was an extreme shortage of qualified personnel for wartime communications in 1944. Repeated nationwide announcements on the radio begged for licensed radio operators to serve on merchant ships. Merchant Marine ships were used to transport troops and cargo to dangerous war zones in the Atlantic and Pacific Oceans. These ships carried troops, tanks, guns, landing craft, ammunition, oil, and supplies. Liberty ships were produced in large numbers. Faster Victory ships came later.

Now that I had my FCC licenses, I was qualified to apply to serve aboard a ship. There I could assume responsibilities for communications, including the maintenance of receivers and transmitters, and ship-to-ship and ship-to-shore communications using Morse code.

While on my way home to Kenosha, I thought about enlisting in the Merchant Marine. I had heard a rumor that I wouldn't need much of a physical. I considered the dangers I would face with German submarines, known as U-boats, lurking in the North Atlantic, where they were sinking hundreds of American and Allied ships. I also knew I could be assigned to the known dangers of the Murmansk run to Russia over the top of Norway near the Arctic where German submarines and planes waited and bombed and torpedoed ships. There was a 50 percent chance of surviving a mission destined for a Russian port, and afterward, a 50 percent chance of returning to the point of origin. I knew the risks, but I didn't want to be left behind with the women and children. I was nearly twenty, and wanted to serve my country. Many of my friends were risking their lives, so why shouldn't I?

Boarding the SS *Sidney Lanier*

There is no doubt there was an immediate dire need for radio personnel. I applied, was approved without a physical examination, and received orders to take a train to arrive in New York City the very next day. McCormick Shipping Lines and the U.S. War Shipping Administration already had made all travel arrangements for me.

I was proud and ready to join with other men and women who were risking their lives for our country. Various national slogans, which all made supreme sense to me, strongly influenced me to join in our war efforts abroad. "This is the war to end all wars" was one; the slogan that most moved my emotions was, "We are fighting for the freedom for our children and their children." My 4-F rating was behind me. I could now take part in our country's wars with Germany and Japan. I left home, leaving my mother, stepfather, and my two brothers. My mother cried when I left, wishing I had not enlisted.

On the train from Kenosha to Chicago to New York City, I had my own berth with a bunk bed in first-class style. As soon as I arrived in New York City, I took a cab to McCormick Shipping Lines offices located in lower Manhattan. While in New York, I constantly looked up at the many tall buildings, including the Empire State Building. Anybody who saw me could easily tell I was a "hick" and not a New Yorker, I'm sure.

I arrived at McCormick office. I obviously was really a green "rookie." The first mistake I made was my response to these instructions for getting to my ship, "Go to the end of Broadway, and then take a ferry to Staten Island."

"What is a ferry?" I asked.

I recall explicitly to this day exactly what he answered, "What is a ferry!? Don't you know?" Then, in a deriding tone, he said, "It's a boat."

I was embarrassed but a little angry with him. I now wish I would have said to him, "Hey, tell me what a ferry is. I'm from Kenosha. Do you know where Kenosha is?"

There wasn't time for training. I hadn't received any training at Sheepshead Bay, the major U.S. Maritime Training Center in New York, or at King's Point, where U.S. Maritime officers were trained, or at the U.S. Coast Guard, or anywhere else. I was deemed ready to go. I was excited as I looked forward to boarding a ship for my first voyage ever.[3]

I was taken to the ship on a pilot boat. A pilot boat is used to bring in a pilot to steer the ship toward land and a dock or shore point due to the pilot's intimate knowledge of the waters and underwater obstructions. The goal is to avoid a collision that would damage the ship's hull. Anyway, I was brought to my ship. I also had my trunk of personal belongings.

While being brought to my ship, I met another man on the boat being brought to another ship. He asked, "Have you ever sailed before?"

I answered, "No, this is my first trip."

"I thought so," he said. "You look like you're green. I'll give you some tips. I've been sailing a long time."

I listened attentively while he explained tricks that I could expect to receive for my initiation. His advice really helped. One trick that I remember was that I would be asked if I had ever seen the golden stream on the ship and what would happen if I said, "No." Therefore, I didn't go to the bottom of our ship so I could see the "golden stream," bend over to look for it, and then get booted in the rear end. I saved myself a trip through the engine room and a kick in the rear and seamen laughing at me.

The pilot boat brought me to the side of the SS *Sidney Lanier*, where there was a rope ladder for me to take up to the main deck. I looked up to the railing, took a deep breath, and climbed up the long ladder. My trunk remained in the pilot boat. I had been previously informed I would be a warrant officer for the first six months and then

---

[3] For more about Sheepshead Bay, visit www.usmm.org/sheepsheadbay.html. For training of officers and gun crews, visit www.usmm.net/gunnery.html.

promoted to an ensign's rank in the U.S. Maritime Service if I received good ratings from the captain.

As I was reaching the top and was thinking about my rank, I learned something quickly. I thought I would use my rank—about which I knew nothing, not having received any training—and ordered a seaman standing on the deck, "Say, take up my trunk." He had no idea who I was, and sarcastically replied using only two words as an expletive of full rejection.

Fortunately, the boatswain mate, a captain's assistant in charge of the ship's sailors, was standing nearby. He heard the conversation and asked me, "Are you our new sparks?" Sparks was an expression used for a ship's radio operators. I said, "Yep."

He shook my hand and said, "Welcome!" Then, he yelled out at the seaman who had not greeted me cordially, "Take up the trunk." He did as ordered and pulled my trunk up to the main deck and carried it to my room located on the deck below the top deck. I met the ship's Chief Radio Officer Ensign John Shakespeare.

John, who looked to be at least twenty-five, came from a wealthy English family who lived in the United States. John carried his weight as that of a wealthy individual with a superior attitude. He gave me the impression that many of the seamen were just peons. His first reaction to me as his new assistant was not one of superiority in this sense, but more like, "You young punk, how much am I going to have to teach you?" We had a U.S. Navy radioman too, a member of the U.S. Naval Armed Guard, who sailed on our ship to man the guns.

I overlooked John's superior attitude and we got along just fine. Shakespeare set up our schedules for duty, customarily four hours on and eight off, for each of us. I was not scheduled to work my first shift until the next morning. I had my own private room and slept in a bunk bed attached to the bulkheads (walls). I turned in for the night. I was filled with dread that our ship could be sunk by torpedoes and, at the same time, a sense of adventure. I hadn't been told when we were leaving, and I didn't ask.

My First Voyage: The Largest Convoy in History

The next morning I woke up, stepped outside of my room on to the deck, and saw with wide-eyed astonishment that we were out at sea! We had departed from our dock position in darkness. It was now early morning and we were in the Atlantic Ocean. I didn't expect it so soon. We had joined up with dozens of other ships all converging into a convoy that filled the ocean from horizon to horizon. A spectacular sight! We had departed during the night of May 9, 1944.

I had seen the radio room when I met Shakespeare. It looked about the same as I expected--a large transmitter and two radio receivers built into the wall, a typewriter, counter to write on, two chairs and a Morse code "key" on the counter. The room measured about eight by nine feet, with an attached room about the size of a walk-in closet that contained banks of batteries (similar to car batteries) in the event of power failure.

We sailed in a convoy so our escorts could provide concentrated protection against attack by German submarines, which had destroyed many single cargo ships in North Atlantic and European waters. German U-boats sunk approximately twenty-five hundred ships during World War II. Our escorts included Canadian Corvettes with sonar equipment to detect subs below. Convoys not only protected ships against attacks in the Atlantic away from our eastern coast but also discouraged U-boat attacks on ships near our eastern borders. A convoy offered a mass of protection for ships. To ensure the stability of a convoy, if a ship was torpedoed or bombed, or hit an explosive mine, other ships continued on without stopping to aid survivors of the disabled or sinking ship.

Our convoy included Liberty ships, oil tankers, and ammunition ships, as well as Canadian Corvettes, prepared to drop depth charges on German submarines. Liberty ships carried war equipment and supplies. There were many advantages to sailing in a convoy. However, a distinct disadvantage was that a convoy could only move on the waters as fast as the slowest ship. In the case of convoys with Liberty ships, the fastest speed allowed was only 9 knots (a nautical measurement) per hour, equivalent to about 10 miles per hour.

After several hours, the ship began to move gently to and fro. While I was on duty, the captain poked his head into the radio room. He was smoking a light brown corncob pipe, a man in his fifties with gray hair. He greeted me, saying, "I'm Captain Stegen.

I replied, "I'm glad to meet you, Captain Stegen. Then I said, "It's really rough out here, Captain."

He laughed deeply, and then said, "Rough? This isn't rough! It's like living in a hotel."

I sure didn't think so, but I didn't disagree with him. Well, in about four or five days, I knew what he meant. We were hit by a North Atlantic storm.

I soon learned that a storm in the North Atlantic could be ferocious. A storm would last for fifteen days or more or for as little as two or three days. During a storm, one would roll in his bunk bed but would eventually learn to sleep through it. Dishes with solid foods on them had to be held while eating; objects that could be thrown into midair had to be tied down. It was difficult to hold your sea legs (walk and not fall) without hanging on to the bulkhead railing on the inside ship's hallway walls or deck railings.

And then there would be those who would become seasick in the rough weather. I was fortunate not to get seasick. Occasionally, when the weather would be extremely rough, I would have a slightly decreased sense of smell, even for good food, or my equilibrium would be affected a little. Otherwise, I was just fine. I didn't ever need to vomit on my ocean voyages.

As an assistant radio officer, I had my room on the top deck near the captain's quarters. My room was small. Chief Radio Officer Shakespeare had a larger room on the same deck. Our captain was the supreme commander on ship. His quarters included a large sleeping room, a study area, and a conference room. There were a few occasions during my voyages when I heard the captain reprimand and warn a seaman in his quarters. I didn't know or hear of any severe reprimands against officers. At the captain's sole discretion, crewmembers could be jailed.

Due to my asthma, I looked forward to my lungs' reaction to the ocean air. I had heard it was very helpful for persons with asthma. I didn't have any breathing problems out at sea the first day, the second day, the third day, or ever again from that point on to this date. A miracle indeed! I'm still slightly allergic to dust, but I have never again had an asthma attack.

Besides Merchant Marine personnel, our ship's personnel also included twenty-five to thirty sailors who served in the U.S. Naval Armed Guard and received their orders from a naval officer aboard our ship who held the rank of lieutenant commander. He gave orders to these sailors for manning and operating the guns aboard ship. Depending on the ship, we would have a number of 20-millimeter guns, and either a 3-inch, 4-inch, or 5-inch gun on both our bow and our stern. The type and size of a ship determined the size and number of its guns.

The Navy lieutenant commander reported to the ship's captain. Men on ships were extremely loyal to our purpose and cause. All worked as a team. President Roosevelt and General MacArthur bestowed honors upon us in their famous statements *(see Chapter 8)* about the Merchant Marine, Maritime Service, and Armed Guard during World War II.

Destination Unknown

Merchant ships that left U.S. ports did not know their destination when they departed. This was highly confidential military information. Not even the captains knew their destinations until near their arrival point.

At sea, many precautions were necessary to block detection by German U-boats as much as possible. Beside our blackouts at night, we observed complete radio silence day and night. Telegraph signals at high frequencies for long distance communications and radio signals at low frequencies for communication from ship to ship or ship to shore were prohibited except in extreme emergencies. There were no limits on receiving messages.

For ship-to-ship communication during daylight hours, signalmen could communicate with each other using blinking light signals or flags. Each ship carried a large powerful encased lamp attached to the deck with a shutter on it to interrupt its powerful light for measured intervals to represent letters and words. For flag messages, a sailor would hold a large flag in each hand and place them in certain positions on his body or near his body to represent letters and words.

Blackout rules went into effect as soon as it became dark. All lights on deck were turned off. Lights of any kind were not allowed on the outside of the ship. Only dim red lights were used in the hallways, as these faint lights could not be seen from the outside of the ship.

As radiomen, we kept a log twenty-four hours per day throughout the entire trip. The operator on duty typed his entry every fifteen minutes to record any signals heard. Because we rarely ever received signals, sheet after sheet of our reports showed "No Signals Heard." We were not allowed to send any signals or messages by telegraph or radio except SOS (Save Our Ship) on the captain's order if our ship started to sink for any reason, such as hitting a mine or getting hit by a torpedo, and then only if we were not in a convoy.

Our secret codebook was kept in a fairly large heavy steel box with a strong padlock. All sides and the top and bottom of the box contained holes. The purpose of the holes was to force the box to sink in the event a torpedo or bomb hit our ship or we hit a mine. In such an event, it was the chief radio officer's duty to dump the box with its holes overboard. This box was kept in our locked battery room, which also contained batteries to supply power to our transmitter and our radio receiver.

Each ship was identified by four secret call letters. Messages were transmitted in code to our secret call letters. All messages that included secret coded messages were received by telegraph over long distances in Morse code, not by radio over short distances. Destinations were transmitted to us from the Broadcast for Allied Merchant Ships, or BAMS, when we were near Great Britain.

John Shakespeare assumed full responsibility for the radio room and the codebooks. I recall that all BAMS messages came from Boston with their powerful transmitters. John also had responsibility for all of the equipment in the radio room, including the repairs and maintenance of the transmitter, receivers and batteries in the battery room. Later, when I became a radio officer, I assumed these responsibilities.

As we drew nearer and nearer to Great Britain, we waited anxiously to learn whether we would be ordered to Murmansk, a death-defying route for cargo ships and the naval ships protecting them.

Murmansk is located on the Kola Gulf in the Barents Sea in Russia. It is 625 miles north of St. Petersburg, and about 35 miles from the open sea. It is the largest city in the world north of the Arctic Circle. The port is ice free, and is kept open all winter by warm currents flowing up from the Gulf Stream. Due to the strategic importance of these supply lines, as well as the fierce German resistance and extreme weather conditions that plagued the area, the merchant mariners and Navy sailors who sailed on the "Murmansk Run" are considered some of the bravest veterans in history.

On or about May 25, 1944, we received the first BAMS message regarding our destinations. John listened with his earphones until he heard our ship's call letters, and recorded the message received in secret code. I stood by. We held our breath. It was not Murmansk! We were ordered to proceed to Glasgow, Scotland. John brought notice of our destination to our captain immediately. We felt relieved.

After first stopping at Cromarty Firth in Scotland, we proceeded to Glasgow and arrived there on June 5, 1944. At this time of the year in the far north, the nights were very short. We had only two to three hours of darkness. While off duty and on shore, I enjoyed mixing with the Scots, who always treated us with respect, and had an occasional date with a pretty Scottish girl.

My first date ever was in Glasgow. I was finally able to afford to take a girl out to dinner. We walked to a fine restaurant. This restaurant had an excellent menu with choices of vegetables in particular. At the time, meats, fruits, and vegetables were in short supply and expensive in Scotland and all of Great Britain. Even salads were rare. I don't recall her main entree or mine, but I remember she explained the shortage of lettuce and tomatoes and how she liked lettuce and tomatoes. She was thrilled with her salad! This introduction to a Glasgow restaurant and my dinner with this fine young lady are a pleasant memory.

A couple of our ship's officers and I visited different attractions in Glasgow. We also visited stores, restaurants, and museums; took bus rides; and didn't forget to shop. I bought a fine set of beautifully painted teacups and plates for my mother as a memory of my trip.

While in Scotland, I also visited Edinburgh, not far from Glasgow. To get there we used a tram, their word for a train. In my opinion, Edinburgh is one of the most beautiful cities to see. It has colorful hills and vales, and brick structures painting the landscape. My ship friend and I visited castles and museums. Their castles are absolutely beautiful. I think their most popular castle is Edinburgh Castle, which has stood for hundreds of years and is proudly maintained. As everywhere else, Scottish people respected American servicemen immensely for our war efforts against Germany.

We left Glasgow on June 19, 1944, following my twentieth birthday on June 18, and returned to New York. During wartime, cargo ships did not return goods of any kind back to the United States. Therefore, due to the lack of cargo, the ship's main deck would be many feet higher on the water and much lighter than on the way over.

We arrived in New York City on July 5, 1944. While waiting for the ship to be loaded again for my next trip, I took a plane and returned home to visit my family and relatives. We were overjoyed to see one another. I gave Mom the teacup set I had purchased in Scotland. She was thrilled and delighted with my thoughtfulness. After she passed away, this beautiful tea set remained a family treasure.

I visited a number of our relatives and friends in Kenosha. As they honored me, I was grateful for their love and kindness. They couldn't seem to do enough for me in terms of their hospitality and their warmth, and, as always, I enjoyed a plentiful supply of their home-baked items and special dishes.

Being back home on land, I decided it was a good time to contact International Correspondence School, or ICS, and enroll in a cost accounting Course. ICS was regarded as the most outstanding correspondence school in our country. Because most people couldn't afford college costs, correspondence courses were considered an excellent way to enhance one's knowledge. I enrolled and received textbooks and study assignments before I left Kenosha for my next voyage.

One of the best educational decisions I made in my lifetime was to enroll with ICS and study accounting during the war while out at sea. We did not have movies, tape players, or VCRs, so there wasn't much to do when not on duty. There wasn't anywhere to go, either. Other officers and I passed some of our time playing pinochle, our favorite and only card game, in the officers' mess hall almost every day. We became very good pinochle players. We also read fiction and non-fiction books, exchanging many well-known and popular books with one another. A favorite at the time was *A Tree Grows in Brooklyn*. We also had many copies of magazines. My favorite was the *Reader's Digest*. At that time, the digest only contained articles—no advertising whatsoever. It was a pleasure. And I had hundreds of free hours for studying and completing my assignments. The knowledge I received from these studies has helped throughout my entire life.

My Second Atlantic Voyage

After enjoying visiting my family and friends, I returned to New York City and returned to the SS *Sidney Lanier*. We left July 25, 1944, sailing in a large convoy again. I was appointed chief radio officer by the captain and put in charge of two U.S. Navy operators. If there would be any problems with these radiomen, I would discuss such problems with their lieutenant commander. For example, one of the radiomen drank quite a bit when we were on shore and would get drunk. He did not create any problems in the radio room, but I was concerned that if he would enter a vacant radio room while drunk, he could "screw up our transmitter or receivers." Radiomen could enter the room but were not authorized to open up the transmitter or receiver panels. As Radio Officer, I had sole control of the transmitter and receiver.

During our journey, we had a scare. I heard a very loud explosion that severely rocked our ship. I thought for sure that a torpedo had hit us. I remained in the radio room waiting for the captain's orders. But we had not been hit; a depth charge had been dropped close to our ship by one of our Corvettes to explode an enemy submarine in the water below. We continued on and had a safe trip the rest of the way.

As we neared our unknown destinations, per orders received from BAMS, I deciphered and reported the instructions to Captain Stegen. We proceeded to Oban, Scotland, and arrived there on August 8, 1944, and then to Copenhagen, Denmark. Copenhagen was filled with friendly people. Our ship docked at a large pier. We did not need to go back and forth to our ship with a small boat as we did when our ship was anchored in the water near land.

We enjoyed their streets and restaurants. I remember the statute of the little mermaid on the shore waters, one of their main attractions. Their churches, and castles, and architecture were a sight to behold. We remained in Copenhagen for a while and then departed, sailing in the North Sea and arriving in South End on the Thames River near London on September 16, 1944.

We anchored in the Thames for a few days. We were waiting to cross the English Channel to deliver war goods to ports in northern France used by Allied forces on D-Day, including Utah Beach and Cherbourg. Rockets headed for London passed over our ships regularly. These rockets fired into London from the mainland of Germany were V-1s. They traveled at speeds of 400 miles per hour only a few hundred feet above ground level and not much higher than our ship's mast. Most of them landed in the London area and the southern part of England, creating large areas of devastation and havoc.

The first bomb that passed very closely past our ship after we had anchored was almost mast high. At the time, I was in the head (the bathroom), standing near the toilet. I heard a loud roar close overhead, and I reacted with a sudden jerk of my body. I wish I had not been standing and urinating when I jerked from the roaring noise.

These German rockets were intentionally aimed at cities and towns to kill women and children, hoping to destroy Great Britain's strong will to fight. English men, women, and children showed an immense amount of courage and fortitude while they were bombed day after day. Food supplies were low. Bomb shelters were everywhere. While waiting in London, my shipmates and I visited many of London's damaged buildings and bomb shelters as well as many of the famous landmarks.

London's people did not crumble and survived many months of constant bombings. At this time, the Germans were sending over new V-2 rockets that traveled at faster speeds with more explosive power than the V-1s. Many smaller cities and towns on the southern coast of England adjacent to the English Channel had been destroyed.

On to France, Then Back to the United States

From London, we then sailed to Yarmouth on England's south coast. A few days later, we left Yarmouth and joined with a number of other ships. We sailed with heavy protection by U.S. destroyer escorts as we crossed into northern France where we unloaded our tanks, guns, and equipment at Utah Beach and Cherbourg. Utah Beach and Cherbourg clearly showed destruction in the aftermath of D-Day. I felt a huge sense of gratitude and appreciation for our country's massive strength as these destroyers cut through the waters of the English Channel, protecting us and our valuable cargo.

Our ship was anchored a short way from shore. While our ship was being unloaded and our cargo was brought to land, we became acquainted with the French. They did not have much food. Their houses were away from the beachheads. While on land one day, as the day was ending, a girl who owned a beautiful angora kitten walked me to my small boat, which ferried crewmen back to the ship anchored nearby. She pleaded with me to bring the kitten with me aboard ship because she did not have enough food to feed her pet. Therefore, I hid the kitty in my officer's coat and brought it on the ship to my room. I made a place for her in a corner of my room. Of course, pets were prohibited on board. But since I had my own private room and hardly anyone ever entered my room, except my steward, I thought that no one would find out. I would see to it that my door was always kept closed. My steward cleaned my room daily and made my bed for me, as was customary for all officers. I secretly informed him I had a kitten in my room, and asked him to clean up the kitten's box and not to tell anyone. Stewards always accommodated ship officers to earn handsome tips at the end of a voyage.

The next day, my steward notified me the kitten had left the room and walked up to the top deck and climbed on to the captain's mattress. The captain slept there during violent storms or in emergencies. He explained to me the kitten had soiled the mattress and that he tried to wash the soiled areas but could not get rid of the stains or the smell. Therefore, he replaced it with a new mattress and threw the soiled mattress overboard. I said to him, "Good job. Nice going. Thanks very much."

Officers ate in a "mess hall," at assigned tables, and were served breakfast, lunch, and dinner. Four officers sat at each table. I was the youngest officer, and sat at the end table, furthest from the captain, with three other officers.

During our dinner this day, the captain asked, "Does anyone here know anything about a mattress I saw overboard when I was coming back to our ship?" I thought Oh, Oh. I was really in for it now.

I spoke up, and said, "Yes, Captain. I know. I had a kitten that I should not have had, and it messed your mattress."

He replied, "I'll tell you once. Get rid of that cat in the morning immediately; otherwise, I will throw it overboard, and you will be hanging on to it."

I replied, "Yes sir." I brought the kitty back to the beach and let it go. I heard someone say, "Somebody is going to have a fine dinner."

While we remained in France, one of our officers who had worked as a reporter for the *Washington Post* asked to meet with me in confidence. He asked me if I could set up a microphone in a secret hiding place on our ship. We had a radio speaker located in our officers' mess hall and one or two for the crewmembers in their area. He wanted to write up and host fictional newscasts about imaginary events occurring back in the states that would be very interesting and entertaining for officers and crewmembers. He promised he would not interfere with regular news broadcasts we received on our ship's radio when near land; we didn't have portable radios then. I didn't see any harm in such a plan and therefore secretly set up a microphone in a secluded area behind a bulkhead (wall) on my deck near my radio room where he could not be seen or heard.

He was a clever writer with an excellent imagination for creating sensational and interesting newscasts for listeners. He was an experienced radio reporter, and spoke very well. His newscasts, heard only on our ship, suddenly became very popular. Of course, shipmates could not confirm if these stories back in the States were true because we did not have contact with the States' newspapers or the ability to receive radio broadcasts from the States due to the distance involved.

I don't recall all of the subjects he covered, but I remember that his first newscast included a special bulletin regarding "the White Rose Killer" in Boston. I will describe three examples as I can best recall them:

"Boston! The White Rose Killer has struck again. Police discovered the body of a woman on the fourteenth floor of a prominent hotel in Boston. This is the sixth murder of a woman by the White Rose Killer and police are baffled. He again left his signature: a white rose placed on the bosom of the victim. Women are cautioned to be careful with strangers and not to enter a room alone with a stranger."

"Miami! Miami has taken the first step in America to introduce the comfort and nudity of women on beaches. Hundreds of women have appeared on the beach without bathing suit tops, causing a backlash by many citizens regarding their lack of decency. Citizens are objecting, but women continue to walk the beaches showing their bare bosoms. I will keep you fully informed in my special newscasts."

"New York City! Today, in the (famous restaurant name) Billy Conn, the best light heavyweight champion of all time, who nearly defeated heavyweight champion Joe Louis in their last fight, accidentally bumped into a puny five-feet-eight-inch restaurant patron who weighed less than 140 pounds. He stood up to Billy's face and threatened to hit Billy smack between the eyes. Billy dared him! He hit Billy in the face with a right hand and knocked him to the floor! Billy got up staggering and sat down in his chair. Billy later said, 'I'm not shaken up one bit.'"

Each broadcast lasted only ten minutes. He and I were the only two who knew these broadcasts were fake stories. I was amazed to observe our shipmates who eagerly huddled near a radio to listen to his broadcasts at their scheduled time each day.

After a week or so, I noticed our ship's chief engineer walking on my deck. His appearance on a top deck was unusual. Chief engineers rarely came up to my upper deck. Their work involved our ship's engines, all located below the main deck. It turned out that he became suspicious about these special newscasts. He decided to see if these spectacular and unbelievable newscasts we coming from within our ship for fun. He discovered the microphone behind the wall. He came to my radio room and asked me if I had set it up. He figured it out. Of course, I admitted I had. No further broadcasts were made from that day on. Many of our crewmembers laughed when they learned these broadcasts were a hoax. The captain never addressed this matter, and no one expressed a complaint.

After we unloaded our ship in northern France, we then sailed to Falmouth and departed from there on October 31, 1944. We arrived safely back in New York on November 17, 1944.

We had been away from the States for four months. I returned home in time for the Christmas holidays with my mother, father, and brother Vince as I waited for my next assignment in San Francisco on a Victory ship. My brother Emil was away serving in the U.S. Army. I also visited with my friends and relatives, enjoying our association and get-togethers.

One of my best friends, Wally Bauer, who served in the U.S. Air Force, was also home on leave. We spent time together visiting some of our favorite night spots. For example, we went to the Eagles Club, where we had a drink or two and met with some people we knew. We also went to the VFW bar. We were not big drinkers, but liked to socialize.

My Christmas at home in 1944 was full of joy. I was very happy to be home to enjoy our fine dinners, Christmas songs, and church services. I spent time with my family in a traditional manner, with special delicacies. As usual, we exchanged visits with a neighbor or two and shared our tables full of many specially prepared foods and homemade cookies.

I had made a date with Joyce, a pretty girl in my hometown, to take her to a midnight mass on Christmas Eve at St. James, a Catholic church nearby. She agreed I could come to her home to pick her up at about 10:00 p.m. with Wally. We met her parents and family members and stayed a while. Then we left for mass. I brought her home and made another date with her. I also had a date with a different girl from my high school class. I see her at our high school reunions to this day and exchange pleasantries.

Chapter 8: Praise for the Merchant Marine

Here are some comments from the president and others about the Merchant Marine. Unless otherwise noted, the quotations come from www.usmm.org/quotes.html, the U.S. Maritime Service Veterans' Web site.

President Franklin D. Roosevelt, September 19, 1944: "It seems to me particularly appropriate that Victory Fleet Day this year should honor the men and management of the American Merchant Marine. The operators in this war have written one of its most brilliant chapters. They have delivered the goods when and where needed in every theater of operations and across every ocean in the biggest, the most difficult and dangerous transportation job ever undertaken. As time goes on, there will be greater public understanding of our merchant fleet's record during this war."

Gen. Douglas MacArthur, October 14, 1945: "I wish to commend to you the valor of the merchant seamen participating with us in the liberation of the Philippines. With us they have shared the heaviest enemy fire. On this island I have ordered them off their ships and into fox holes when their ships became untenable targets of attack. At our side they have suffered in bloodshed and in death. The caliber of efficiency and the courage they displayed in their part of the invasion of the Philippines marked their conduct throughout the entire campaign in the southwest Pacific area. They have contributed tremendously to our success. I hold no branch in higher esteem than the Merchant Marine…They have brought us our lifeblood and they had paid for it with some of their own. I saw them bombed off the Philippines and in New Guinea ports. When it was humanly possible, when their ships were not blown out from under them by bombs or torpedoes, they have delivered their cargoes to us who needed them so badly. In war it is performance that counts." (*Author's note: From a news release from the War Shipping Administration, Washington Advance Release Sunday Papers.)*

Gen. Dwight D. Eisenhower, 1945: "The officers and men of the Merchant Marine, by their devotion to duty in the face of enemy action, as well as the natural dangers of the sea, have brought us the tools to finish the job. Their contribution to final victory will be long remembered."

Bob Hope, Christmas 1944 broadcast to the Merchant Marine: "They're Z-men. Did you ever hear of Z-men? Sounds like a gag, doesn't it? Well, it isn't. Z-men are the guys without whom General Ike's army and Admiral Nimitz's navy couldn't live. Five thousand seven hundred of them have died from enemy torpedoes, mines, bombs, or bullets since our zero hour at Pearl Harbor.

"Z-men are the men of the Merchant Marine. They carry a big wad of identification papers in a book called a Z book, so they call them Z-men...Listen, it takes nerve to go to work in a hot engine room, never knowing when a torpedo might smash the hull above you and send thousands of tons of sea water in to snuff out your life. It takes courage to sail into the waters of an enemy barbaric enough to tie your hands and feet and submerge you so you can drown, like a rat, without a fight. It takes courage to man an ammunition ship after you heard how Nazi bombers blew up 17 shiploads of ammunition at Bari and not a man was ever found of the crews. I was there about that time. I'll never forget it."

New York Times, June 9, 1944, from London: "D-Day would not have been possible without the Merchant Marine. Now that the long-awaited day is history and great Allied forces have been landed in France, it is permitted to indicate the part played by these intrepid civilians, whose deeds for the most part have gone unsung. It is not generally realized that the Merchant Marine has the largest ratio of casualties of any branch of the services, and many of the names on the list are not classified 'wounded' or 'missing.' They were those of the men whose grave is the sea.

Mom and Dad with
Emil (L) and Me - 1928

My Mom on her farm near town - 1950
She raised her own chickens and vegetables.
We all loved her cooking.

Brother Emil (L) and Me in World War II - 1944

Ensign Sam S. Ruffalo - U.S. Maritime Service
Served overseas in World War II;
Honorably discharged by U.S. Coast Guard.

My first wife,
Mary Ann Ruffalo - 1952

Mary Ann, Lynn, and baby Randy - 1957
My son - he was an angel.

Some of the Ruffalos - 1961
Front: Diane, Richard, Lynn, and Randy
Back: Louise, Grandma Ruffalo, Mary Ann, and Me

Lynn and Randy - 1966

Me, Lynn, and Mary Ann - 1966

(L-R) Mary Ann, Sister-in-Law Louise,
Me, and Brother Emil - 1970

More Ruffalos (L-R): Louise, Lynn, Bob, Mary Ann,
Friend, Diana, Randy, Richard, and Emil - 1973

One of my top insurance agents, Ralph Kratochvil,
with his wife at one of our dinners - 1960s

Me receiving a plaque as President
of Hales Corner's Chamber of Commerce - 1972
Officers present (L-R): Dave O'Brien, Me, Don Diven, and
Chamber Secretary

The three Ruffalo brothers - 1972
(L-R) Me, Emil, and Vince

Lynn in her first marriage to Robert Jaeger

Bob honors Lynn for earning her BSN degree
from the University of Wisconsin-Milwaukee

Ground breaking for my office building at
3380 S. 108th Street, Greenfield, Wisconsin – 1972

Chapter 9: Sailing in the Pacific

After I returned to the U.S. East Coast, I asked to be assigned to a Victory ship in the Pacific Ocean. The Pacific wasn't much safer in regards to the war, but its waters were nowhere near as turbulent as the ferocious, storm-plagued seas of the North Atlantic.

My wish was granted. I was given instructions to proceed to San Francisco after New Year's Day, 1945. After my arrival, I was assigned to the *S.S. Elko Victory.* I knew we would sail alone; convoys were not used in the Pacific.

I also knew that Victory ships sailed at 17 knots per hour, almost twice the speed of Liberty cargo ships and twice the speed of submarines under water. This knowledge added comfort. As usual, no one really knew our destination, but we could guess. I had no idea that I would be assigned to sail on an ammunition ship! We carried five-hundred-pound bombs and guessed our destination would be an Air Force base.

As we left shore, I recall thinking is that if our ship would get hit by a torpedo or bomb, I would never know it, so I didn't need to worry about it.

Aboard the SS Elko Victory

Sailing in the Pacific without escorts would take time despite the faster speed of our ship. That's because our ship changed direction frequently to confuse any submarines. We could go forward and then zigzag to the left or zigzag to the right one time, and then a different direction and right back again, or take a different zigzag pattern altogether, never following an expected direction for a Japanese sub to get in a position to torpedo us.

Our captain's name was Captain Westerlund. He was husky and appeared tougher with crewmembers than Captain Stegen. We left San Francisco on January 19, 1945.

This voyage to the Far Pacific and back took four months. We were lucky not to have been torpedoed or bombed by any planes or to have struck a mine. Although Japanese planes strafed us, we received minor damage and no injuries while anchored in the Philippines. Our ship's gunners did their job well. But at times, a 20-millimeter gun would hit one of my radio room's antenna wires. Crewmembers easily replaced the wires, and we would kid around and say, "At least they hit something."

The Japanese did not target cargo ships or oil tankers in the Pacific as a rule in early 1945. However, Japanese subs did torpedo and destroy many merchant ships at Pacific island beahheads in 1942 and 1943. Countless other cargo ships were damaged by kamikaze planes, bombers, artillery, and torpedoes during landing operations by the United States Marine Corps as those soldiers were reaching island ports for invasions.

Shortly after we arrived safely at New Guinea, we traveled to the Solomon Islands, then on to Leyte in the Philippines for a few days, and then to Clark Field, our U.S. Air Force base in Manila.

Sad News by Mail: Mother has Colon Cancer

While at Clark field, our mail was passed out. I received a letter with the sad news that my mother was diagnosed with colon cancer. I was informed that she was not expected to live for more than six months. I wept in my room knowing that perhaps I would never be able to see my mom again. I had lost my father due to cancer of the colon, now I would lose my mother. With the graces of God and prayer, her colostomy was successful and she survived. On my next trip home, I gave her extra hugs.

A Most Valuable Non-combat Commodity

We unloaded all of our bombs at Clark Field; B-29s used them to continue bombing the Japanese mainland. One day, I noticed that military police were guarding our ship during unloading. I wondered why they were there. It turned out they were to prevent pilferage of the hundreds of cases of beer being unloaded from the ship.

We left Tacloban, Leyte, for home on May 5, 1945. It began to strongly appear the United States was beginning to win the war against Japan, but unfortunately there were heavy losses of and injuries to servicemen in the Marines and Army. We left Manila and after sailing approximately six thousand miles back across the Pacific, we arrived in Portland, Oregon, on May 26, 1945. In all, we had sailed twenty thousand miles. We remained onboard to prepare for our next voyage.

Chapter 10: World War II Ends!

We remained on ship in Portland while it was loaded, then left for San Francisco. We waited there longer than usual for instructions. I didn't customarily inspect the large wooden cases placed into the ships holds, so I wasn't sure of our cargo. Such cases usually carried civilian goods. We left San Francisco on August 6, 1945, and proceeded to the Panama Canal on the Pacific side to cross into the Atlantic Ocean.

En route to the Canal Zone, we received overwhelmingly joyous news over the radio that our war with Japan had ended with the dropping of a second atomic bomb in Japan, on August 9. The first atomic bomb had been dropped in Japan on August 6. Japan's Emperor Hirohito announced the country's unconditional surrender August 15. We had won our war with Germany on VE Day, May 8. World War II was over!

We celebrated with loud cheers, hoorays, and a sense of immense joy. But, of course, we could not celebrate with liquor or drinking of any kind; alcohol was not available and not permitted aboard ship at any time. We continued to listen to the radio and to share our celebration with all of America that the war had come to an end. This day was the happiest day of my life.

I felt proud of our country. All Americans united and did all they could do to the best of their ability to help win the war. Millions of women had worked in industry and shops and made a huge contribution to winning the war. Millions of military men and women lost their lives or were seriously injured. With the help of people throughout the world and our strong military alliances, we met our objective and won the war for ourselves, for our children, and their children. Our nation and others showed indomitable strength and a do or die spirit to defeat our enemies. I was glad to be able to do my best and be a part of our country's most important victory. And I felt both very fortunate and thankful to have escaped injury or death.

Heading for South America

After we left Balboa, Panama, on August 16, we were informed that we would travel to New Orleans and then on to New York. We left

New York on September 1, stopped at Trinidad in the Caribbean, and then proceeded on to Rio de Janeiro, Brazil.

I conjectured at the time that because the war had ended, Moore McCormick Lines, our ship's owner, had decided to send us to South American ports. To the best of my recollection, we had not been loaded up with war goods but with civilian goods in large wooden crates. I didn't have access to orders received by the captain. In any case, we were relieved not to be carrying ammunition to strategic war ports. We no longer observed wartime rules of the sea such as a blackout of the lights on our ship, and keeping daily logs regarding signals or military messages.

Bob Holoubek, a third mate ensign, and I developed a fine friendship during this voyage. After we arrived in Rio de Janeiro, we visited retail shops, took bus rides to see the country, enjoyed fine dinners at restaurants, and had a couple of joint dates. We enjoyed Brazil's steakhouses and restaurants. Delicious, tender prime steaks such as porterhouse and T-bone steaks were very cheap in South America compared with the States. We did not worry about "artery cloggers" or cholesterol levels then. I doubt we had ever heard of these terms. We immensely enjoyed meeting and talking with Brazilian businesspeople and shop owners and would visit with them while drinking demitasse. They were extremely cordial and friendly toward us.

While visiting shops and talking with the owners, I began to think about selling their attractive products in our country. They were very low priced, made by natives who lived in the dense forests nearby and worked for only a few cents per hour. I made friends with some store owners. I recorded contact information and notes about their products for reference when I was back in the United States.

Planning for the Future

Among my favorite products were serving trays made with beautiful patterns of butterfly wings laid under the glass and surrounded by an attractive wood. Butterflies were plentiful in the Brazilian forests. Hundreds of natives caught the butterflies, using nets, then would carefully remove the wings and place them gently in piles. These wings came in hundreds of colors and shades and degrees of iridescence. The wings would then be glued onto onionskin paper in a gorgeous symmetrical pattern.

I bought a couple of these butterfly trays and also two hundred eight-by-eleven-inch sheets of butterfly wings patterns. The butterfly patterns glued on these onionskin sheets were very lightweight, and wouldn't take up much space or create a problem with customs upon entering the United States.

We left Rio de Janeiro on September 22, 1945, for Rio Grande do Sul, and traveled a short distance to Montevideo, Uruguay's main port. People there also treated us very well. The city, like Rio de Janeiro, was very clean. People wore dress clothes every day and took great pride in their personal appearance. Men who came to work on our ship for loading and unloading shipping crates arrived in suits, and then changed into work clothes. When they were ready to return home, they changed back into their dress suits. I also recall that filling stations were beautifully painted, appropriately decorated, and maintained in immaculate condition. They appeared similar to a palace, but smaller.

After a few days, we left for Buenos Aires, Argentina. During these years, Peron was dictator of Argentina. Many citizens did not like him and would assemble in front of his castle to show their displeasure. His castle was well protected with guards and military on horseback. Violence was kept to a minimum. We felt we couldn't leave Argentina fast enough and finally left Buenos Aires on October 12 for Boston. We arrived in Boston on November 9, 1945.

My Final Voyage

Bob Holoubek and I remained with the SS *Elko Victory* for our next and last voyage. We boarded on November 10, 1945, in New York. Our ship was loaded again and left New York November 22, 1945. Our itinerary record shows we arrived at our first point, Port-of-Spain in Trinidad and Tobago near northern Venezuela. We left Port-of-Spain on November 29 for Rio de Janeiro, and then went on to Montevideo. We left Montevideo on January 6, 1946, to return home, stopping at Port-of-Spain, Boston, and finally New York City on January 28, 1946.

While in South America, I visited the merchants I had met earlier and discussed importing their products more seriously. Bob Holoubek and I visited friends and many of the same places we had enjoyed on our prior visit. After we arrived in New York, Bob left for his home in Salem, Oregon. I decided to remain in New York a while longer to make an important decision.

Chapter 11: Setting Up Business in New York City

I now was back in the Good Ol' USA. Should I return to Kenosha to attend the University of Wisconsin, or remain in New York City to start an import/export business? After careful consideration, I decided to remain in New York. Within two days of my decision, I rented an office in lower Manhattan at 305 N. Broadway. The World Trade Center Twin Towers were not built until many years later, long after I had left my office and New York City, but the office was only five blocks from their eventual site.

I named my company the Atlantis Trading Company because the name reminded me of the Atlantic Ocean and because lower Manhattan is very close to the Atlantic. My office included two small rooms. I also rented a finished sleeping room, without kitchen privileges, in the attic of a private residence in Brooklyn for six dollars per week. I didn't own a car, so I took a subway each day to and from my office. I ate all my lunches in one of the restaurants near my office and my evening meals in a home that provided tasty home-cooked meals.

Learning the Import/Export Business

I didn't have any experience in an import/export business, so I decided to study hard, work hard, and gain experience as quickly as possible. Two men who owned an import/export company in my office building were my mentors and were very helpful. I started to make connections with manufacturers of U.S. products that I could export. I wrote to my contacts in Brazil and asked for their current prices for their trays with their beautiful butterfly designs.

My office was in a heavy trade and financial area of New York City, one of the largest ports, if not "*the*" largest port, in United States. I was only two or three blocks from Wall Street and the large banks that handled many international trading transactions. I visited international departments in two or three banks to pick their brains. I studied their information and anything else I could get my hands on that pertained to freight forwarding, shipping documents, packing, and transactions. I learned about revocable and irrevocable letters of credits, import tariffs, pro-forma invoices, dollar exchange values, terms used in foreign trade, and much more. We didn't have computers and networks in those days to quickly obtain the tons of information that would have been extremely helpful.

Products I offered for sale to South American merchants included simulated pearls, rebuilt typewriters, Formica for countertops, flooring materials, and miscellaneous general merchandise. The largest order I received was for forty used automobiles. A dealer in Philadelphia was prepared to ship this order but unfortunately, the buyer canceled the order before shipment.

In addition to my exports, I decided it would now be feasible to import butterfly trays and gift items from Rio de Janeiro. But before submitting my first order to this merchant, I decided to first visit two or three buyers for large department stores plus a few smaller gift shops. I found lukewarm interest, but didn't receive any outright orders. I decided to be conservative.

I ordered thirty trays from Brazil. After I received the trays, I placed three in a gift shop that had asked for three trays on consignment. I found that the larger retail stores were not as interested as smaller retail sellers. As a result, my sales were slow, and I ordered only a dozen more trays over a period of weeks. To my surprise, I learned these trays would not be big sellers.

Therefore, I devoted more time to seeking buyers in South America and India for U.S. products. I found exports easier and more profitable than imports. Many gift shops, especially in New York City, a major U.S. shipping port, did most of their own importing anyway.

Boyhood Friend Becomes My Partner

About a year or so after I had started my business, Al Bartolini, my friend from Kenosha, met me at my office to visit and share time together in Manhattan and to tour New York. During his visit, Al became interested in my business interests. Having worked together in Kenosha as partners on our paper routes as kids, he and I became partners again. We rented a large second-floor room with two beds in Brooklyn. We did not have a kitchen or kitchen privileges. Al owned a car, so he and I rode back and forth to our office every day. However, we didn't use the car for transportation in New York or any of its boroughs, especially in Manhattan, due to heavy traffic.

We worked hard. Frankly, we found that it was difficult to generate profits from our efforts. I was only twenty-two, and Al was twenty. We were filled with ambition, but we lacked experience. As I learned during future years, we lacked two very essential elements: capital and good management. Dun and Bradstreet reports and analysis have shown time and time again that most businesses fail due to the lack of these two requirements.

Al and I worked hard together for approximately six months. Then, Al decided to leave for Florida. I was sad to see him go because we were good friends. I recall we corresponded for a short time with each other after he left. But in a year or less, we lost touch with each other. I always missed Al and could not connect with him through our friends in Kenosha.

Sixty years later, my old friend Carl Chiappetti called me to tell me he had spoken with Al Bartolini by phone. Al had asked Carl if he knew my whereabouts. I contacted Al. It was a wonderful telephone reunion. I was sorry to hear that Al was not in good health and therefore wasn't able to carry on a long conversation with me. So, we kept our conversation short, but we spoke regularly. A short time later, in April 2005, my wife and I traveled to Miramar, Florida, not far from Miami, to visit Al and his wife. We had a most wonderful time during our three-day visit. We also met Al's daughter Nancy and her children.

Despite Al's departure, I continued to operate Atlantis Trading Company, determined to succeed. But I was running out of money. I contacted my mother to ask her for a loan. As a loving mother, she placed a mortgage on her two-family income property and sent me five thousand dollars. Now more than ever, I wanted to succeed. I held on to my dream that I would succeed, have enough money to buy a convertible automobile, return home, and drive on the streets in Kenosha with a pretty young lady sitting next to me.

Doing Business as a Plastic Tile Contractor

In addition to exporting goods, I also took an interest in plastic tile and formed another company called Harrow Associates. I started this business because I saw a full-page color ad by the Dow Chemical Company in a consumer magazine advertising plastic tile as the new way to tile walls in bathrooms, showers, and kitchens. There were many advantages with plastic tile over ceramic tile. I located a wholesaler who would sell tile to me as needed. I began my efforts to obtain orders from retailers and consumers to install plastic tile.

I placed a display advertisement in Brooklyn's main newspaper. I began to receive calls from interested homeowners and arranged appointments to show samples, explain the merits of plastic tile, and provide a quotation for installation including cost of materials and labor. I received orders. I hadn't hired a tile installer yet, so I installed the first few orders. Labor costs for plastic tiles were much lower than for ceramic tiles, a real advantage to the consumer. I learned how to install these tiles and then taught an employee I hired. My tile man was named Vito. He installed my kitchen jobs and retail shop jobs. I continued to get jobs for kitchens and bathrooms.

I made personal sales calls to butcher shops and delicatessens up and down the streets of Manhattan. I had developed an attention-getting approach to capture a prospect's full interest and then ask for the order. I made up a small board about eighteen inches square with plastic tile on its surface to show how tile would look on a wall. I also carried a hammer. I would walk into the store, ask for the owner, and introduce myself. I would show the owner my board and quickly explain the advantages of plastic tile over ceramic tile. I would sum up my sales talk by saying "And this tile won't chip, crack, break, dent, discolor or fade. It is easy to keep clean, and it's inexpensive." Then I would hit the tile board hard twice with head of the hammer. The tile didn't crack or dent. Using this approach, I received a few orders immediately.

Leads from Charlie

Vito, my tile man, lived on the East Side. He told me he would ask his friend Charlie, who was well-known on the East Side, to meet me at my office and that perhaps he could get some orders for me. One day when I came into the office, Vito and Charlie were there. Charlie was sitting in my office chair behind my desk with his feet on the desk. I thought, "That's a lot of nerve." As soon as Vito introduced me to Charlie, I didn't hesitate to politely tell him to get off my chair so I could sit down. He understood my message. We talked for a while about my business and Vito's employment.

On a different day, Charlie and I were walking together on North Broadway near my office. I was impressed that two or three well-dressed individuals nodded to Charlie as we passed by. I thought, "What the heck! Do these men know Charlie?" Charlie did not wear suits. I never did learn why some of these men were nodding to Charlie. I didn't know Charlie well enough to ask him who his friends were. I was miffed, but impressed.

As promised, Charlie referred me to a couple of butcher shops. I visited the owners and told them Charlie had sent me. I presented a proposal to each of them and received orders from them. Charlie did not want a commission. He only wanted to be sure I would use Vito to do the work. Each job was worth about $400, or $800 for both jobs, in 1948 dollars, or equal to $6,460 in 2005 adjusted according to the Consumer Price Index (CPI). I asked Charlie for more of these referrals, of course, but didn't get any more. Charlie had tried to obtain more referrals, but could not do so. I expressed my appreciation to him for his efforts.

Time to Return Home to Kenosha

I continued with my tile work and my import/export business. Financially, I was breaking even for a while. However, during three years, I hadn't earned enough to avoid the loss of capital. I decided to close my businesses and return home to Kenosha. I had invested and lost eight thousand dollars, including my mother's five thousand-dollar loan. I wanted to pay my mother back in future years, but she would tell me not to worry about it. It was a sad financial loss I've never forgotten.

I needed fast money so I could buy a car and return home. To do so, I took a job selling WearEver, the original waterless cookware. I conducted a number of home demonstrations during the next six weeks or so. One of my favorite demonstrations was to cook a chocolate cake in twenty minutes in the WearEver frying pan without water or oil, spread whipping cream on it, and serve it. The ladies were amazed and loved it! I also demonstrated how to roast small roasts and vegetables on the stove. They were delicious. I didn't know much about cooking, but I had been taught how to cook these foods easily. After the demonstration was over, I sold as many pots as possible. Then, with their permission, I visited those who had attended the demonstration at their residences and sold more cookware to most of them.

I have good memories about this experience. One time when I knocked at the door, a little red-haired boy opened the door and saw me standing there with a pot. We always brought one with us to the front door to hand it to the lady so she would have it in her hand and not slam the door in our face, so to speak. I asked the little boy, "Is your mother home?" He turned his head and yelled back into the house, "Mom, the Pot Man is here!" This was my title—a laughable memory for me.

While working a short time as the "Pot Man," I saved enough to purchase a cheap 1933 Hudson Terraplane automobile and began my long drive home in early 1949. I drove the turnpike, but I also used other highways in mountainous areas to save on tolls. My old Terraplane was as used a car as a car can get; fortunately it ran for the entire trip. I arrived home safe and sound. The next morning, the car wouldn't run until I had it repaired. It was on its last legs.

Chapter 12: Finding Work Back at Home

I needed a good job fast. I wanted to earn an above-average income with a reputable company. I preferred a sales position that offered immediate commissions rather than an hourly job without the opportunity for additional income. I did have the necessary skills and an FCC license to work at a radio broadcasting station, but such a job was not available for me in Kenosha, and I wanted to stay in the area.

My Sales Position with ICS

While looking in the classified section of our local newspaper, I saw an advertisement by International Correspondence Schools (ICS) for a sales and counseling position. I had learned firsthand that ICS was the best correspondence school in America. I had completed a number of the school's accounting courses, but I had a stronger desire to be in sales than to work for an accounting firm or for a factory as a cost accountant. In sales, I would have the opportunity to increase my income and to make friends.

I replied to the ad, went to ICS's office in downtown Milwaukee, and was interviewed by the Wisconsin manager, Erling Peterson. We spent two to three hours together. He hired me because I was prepared for my interview with him and asked him many excellent questions regarding the position. I was hired as the representative for Kenosha and Racine. Mr. Peterson was about fifty-five years old and had been with ICS about twenty years. When he had showed me some of their monthly newsletter regarding other representatives, I noticed most of them were men over forty with many years of long service. I regarded so many older people working for ICS as a good sign of stability.

Mr. Peterson began to train me on leads we would receive from ICS, which advertised extensively in popular men's magazines such as *Popular Mechanics*. In addition, ICS was an approved school for veterans of World War II under the GI Bill of Rights. Personnel who served in the U.S. Maritime Service or Merchant Marine, including those who served in overseas military landing operations in the Pacific or Atlantic, did not receive veteran benefits under the GI Bill of Rights until Congress passed a law in the 1980s granting all veteran benefits to those who qualified. Then, I qualified, as did many other men who risked their lives during World War II in Pacific and Atlantic war zones.

Mr. Peterson and I made calls together. I closely observed how Mr. Peterson used his counseling skills with our prospects to discuss their objectives and goals before he would recommend and discuss subjects to study and their costs. He was a professional and an intelligent individual with broad experience. I learned a lot about how to conduct an interview with my future prospects. There was helpful persuasion involved to make sales, but not high pressure. He taught me how to make sales. He was an excellent teacher.

He also took me with him on calls to visit the personnel directors in various large companies in Racine. A few of these companies encouraged students to take ICS courses to improve their knowledge and skills. If students requested, ICS would send transcripts to their employer following the satisfactory completion of each examination. There were many ICS students who had improved their positions in these companies as a result of taking a course, and having ICS send progress reports to their employer. Therefore, it would be my job not only to sell correspondence courses to individuals, but also to contact industries and explain our courses and their advantages to their employees. In those years, colleges and vocational schools were not as prevalent and did not have the high attendance that they do today because few people could afford them.

I also took a sales course from ICS covering various subjects. I improved my skills and practiced what I was learning. I worked hard and made many calls and visits to earn more and more commissions. I also possessed a strong competitive spirit to be among the leaders in sales. I enjoyed competition and my desire to excel. Within three or four months, I became and remained No. 2 in sales for the next two years in my region of ten states. We received a monthly company sales bulletin consisting of three pages listing the names, locations, and rankings of ICS representatives in my region. At the end of two years, I left ICS for an excellent opportunity with the government as recommended by Wally Bauer, one of my best friends. While working for ICS, I had truly enjoyed selling correspondence courses and conducting interviews with prospective students. I also enjoyed my role in helping men to prepare for and advance in their jobs or careers.

Joining the U.S. Navy Electronics Department

After my return home from New York, Wally and I had reunited. Wally's dad owned a filling station on Sixtieth Street in our neighborhood, and Wally and his brother worked there part time. Every one on the west side of Kenosha knew of Bauer's filling station. Mrs. Bauer kept her husband company and enjoyed shooting the breeze with customers. All loved Mr. and Mrs. Bauer. When I again met up with Wally, he was attending his final year at the University of Wisconsin to earn a degree in electronic engineering.

After Wally graduated in 1949, he was hired as an engineer for the U.S. Navy Electronics Department by his uncle, Mr. Strope, who was a civilian manager in the electronic department at the Great Lakes Naval Base nearby in Illinois. Wally recommended me to his uncle, and I was hired too. Here I was back in radio receivers and electronics equipment, this time for the U.S. Navy.

There was a weakness in civil service still referred to as the "spoils system" that I feel existed in the electronics department at Great Lakes. The spoils system was used very much in the 1800s to employ persons who supported politicians. Although the system had been remedied to a large degree by congressional acts, higher job grades and pay ranks were given to supervisors or department heads according to the number of civil service employees in their units or their department. If work activities were not increased to keep these new hires busy, the workers repeated their functions over and over. Any suggestions for improvements to increase efficiency were disregarded.

As the months rolled on, I found that I did not like this method of operation because too many persons loafed on the job. I felt that I was accomplishing very little and not meeting any challenges. This way of working was not for me, and decided I would not remain with civil service employment. I don't recall that I told Wally I was leaving for this reason.

Chapter 13: My First Marriage

During the early part of 1952, while at one of our popular dances held at the Eagles Club in Kenosha on Sunday evenings, I met Mary Ann Wilson. She was a pretty young lady who accepted my invitation to dance.

Mary Ann told me that she lived at The Girls Club in Kenosha and had left her small town of Suring, Wisconsin, to find employment. She became employed for the Simmons Company. While looking at her in the dimmed lights of the ballroom, I had a premonition that I would be with her into our elderly years. I visualized her as a beautiful elderly woman with gray hair. It was love at first sight. At the end of the evening, I asked if I could take her home. She said I could if I would also give her girlfriends a ride home. I readily agreed.

A few days later, I called Mary Ann and asked her for a date. She accepted. On our date night, I rang the bell at The Girls Club. An older lady answered the door and welcomed me. She was the matron. She interviewed me, asking my name, where I lived, and my job status. She accepted my answers and told me I would be allowed to take Mary Ann out but she could not be out past 11:00 p.m., and no drinking was allowed on dates. She called Mary Ann on the phone; she came down the stairs. This first date was followed by many more dates.

Months later, I proposed. She accepted and I gave her an engagement ring. We set our wedding date for August 30, 1952, approximately six months after we had met at the Eagles Club. Prior to our marriage, we discussed our choice of religion at length. She wanted to remain Lutheran and get married in a Lutheran church, and I wanted to remain a Catholic and get married in a Catholic church. Eventually, she agreed to try Catholicism and chose to be married at St. James and we received premarital instructions there. I also agreed that if she didn't like the Catholic religion after three years, I would become a Lutheran.

We were married on August 30, 1952, at St. James Catholic Church and held our reception at the VFW Hall in Kenosha. We had a large wedding; in all we had two hundred people, and we received many gifts and hundreds of dollars to start our new life together. We spent our honeymoon in Chicago, because I couldn't afford a honeymoon much further away from Kenosha.

We continued to live in Kenosha for several months. We attended mass every Sunday. After several weeks, I quit my job at the Naval Base as I had planned. Kenosha did not offer many jobs except factory jobs, and I had pledged as a teenager that I would never work at American Motors or in a factory. I didn't have any interest to work in a retail store, either. So we moved to Milwaukee in the latter part of May 1953 and rented a small upstairs apartment in a four-family residence. Mary Ann and I cleaned the steps and hallways for a reduction in our rent at 2711-2713 West National Avenue.

Chapter 14: My Career and My Family Begin

As soon as we moved to Milwaukee, I began to look for a sales position. I had decided I would work only for a large company in hopes of having secure employment. I noticed a newspaper advertisement by Allstate Insurance Company that was captioned, "Earn $800 per Month After 2 Years." In 1953, this amount was considered an excellent income. I applied the next day.

Allstate at that time was located at 808 North Third Street in Milwaukee. When I entered the office, I noticed about forty or fifty fine-looking young men in their business suits in the large front lobby. My expectations to become employed by Allstate suddenly were dampened. As I sat waiting for my turn, I thought to myself, "I'll sit it out, but I have a snowball's chance in h--- to get a job here." Individual interviews went fast, in and out, in and out.

I filled out my application and was eventually called. I was interviewed first by District Sales Manager George Hapferte for about five minutes and then by Sales Manager Ray Horner for not more than two minutes. I was asked one question by each of them: why I thought I would succeed as a sales agent for Allstate. I explained that I had studied a correspondence course about selling, and that that I had sold correspondence courses for International Correspondence Schools. I added that I had an excellent sales record as the No. 2 sales representative for ICS in the middle United States. I was asked, "Do you have anything to show this?"

I replied, "I still have my monthly sales bulletins." I was asked to go home, bring copies of these bulletins back, and leave them with the receptionist.

That night, my wife and I had dinner out while shopping a bit. We returned home about 6:30 p.m. There was a well-dressed man in a dark suit sitting on our front steps. He introduced himself as Roland Wandschneider, Allstate's Milwaukee district manager, otherwise known as Rollie.

He asked if he could speak with my wife and me in our apartment. He asked my wife a few questions, including his most important question: "Mrs. Ruffalo, Sam will be working at night three or four nights a week and will not be home until after 9 p.m. while working in the store for Allstate and perhaps making night calls to see his policyholders at their homes. Will it bother or worry you if he's not home at night until later in the evening?"

I remember very clearly that she said, "No, I'm not worried. As long as he makes good money, that's OK with me."

Rollie was pleased with her answers, and asked me to meet him in his office the next morning at 9:00. He and I spent a good part of the day in his office discussing my new career.

He also brought me to the Sears store at 11337 West Forest Home Avenue where insurance agents worked behind a booth as Allstate insurance agents. Allstate was a subsidiary of Sears, Roebuck. Rollie introduced me to the three agents who were on duty. I was told there were seven agents in all who equally split each week's open shifts. Then Rollie and I returned to his office, where I completed more papers. I was hired by Allstate to start as soon as I became licensed as an insurance agent. I studied for two or three days, then took and passed the State of Wisconsin examination.

During my indoctrination, I learned very soon that the top two Allstate agents in United States, Leo and Viola, were located in Kenosha, my hometown. My application showed Kenosha as my previous location. Later, after I became a recruiter of insurance agents, I reminisced about Leo and Viola and thought it didn't hurt my chances of getting hired that I also came from Kenosha.

I immensely enjoyed my new position and working with the other Allstate agents. They had been with the company two to five years. They were great guys with a competitive spirit and fine families.

After six months, I was promoted to sales office supervisor or SOS to provide sales leadership for the seven or eight other agents in our office in addition to my own work as an agent. We worked behind a large rectangular counter high enough for us to easily write on the counter while talking with our policyholders or applicants. We discussed our insurance plans with prospects and our policyholders and filled out applications, claim forms, and other papers while standing up.

At times, agents would call me the booth manager or, in good humor, the "booth mother." We got along very well and shared social events at each other's homes. Part of my job included conducting Monday morning meetings to discuss sales, underwriting requirements, settlement rules of disputes among agents for commission credits, and other subjects of interest. I received a fixed extra monthly wage from Allstate as supervisor in addition to commissions for my personal insurance sales. Paul Fisher, Bill Meese, Bill Pallowick, Bob Wirt, Lee Kosmatka, and Bob Anderson were terrific individuals to work with. There were two other agents who didn't remain with us very long.

Allstate's management staff worked hard as our leaders and wanted us to be better. Each had a unique way about them that inspired agents toward greater accomplishments. I still remember Rolland Wandschneider, who hired me; Dan Vance, Milwaukee's district sales manager; Bill Schuelke, Sales Manager, always extremely enthusiastic; and William Fanning, the regional director responsible to the home office in Skokie, Illinois. There were others who worked out of the Milwaukee office during my employment with Allstate from 1953 to 1958.

Not very long after I began working for Allstate, I decided to buy a house to build equity rather than have a stack of rent receipts. I knew I didn't have enough money to make the usual required 25 percent down payment for a mortgage. Therefore, I checked real estate ads in the Sunday paper for the sale of a small apartment house that I would hopefully be able to buy on a land contract. After several weeks, I found one for sale by the owner. She required a fifteen-hundred-dollar down payment with the balance to be paid in installments under a land contract. The property was located at 2835 West Kilbourn Avenue in Milwaukee. It was a well-kept, two-story frame home with a fair-sized backyard. It had a lower apartment for my wife and me. In addition, there were two sleeping rooms and a three-room apartment to rent out for income on the second floor.

The problem was I didn't have fifteen hundred dollars for the down payment. But before I submitted my offer to purchase to the seller, I applied for and received approval from the Household Finance Company for a fifteen-hundred dollar loan. I signed the loan papers and received a check for the amount of the loan. I deposited my check immediately and contacted the seller the next day and presented her with my check for the down payment with my written offer. She accepted.

My wife and I quickly moved into the first-floor apartment. We kept the same tenants upstairs. It all went well there. In the summer months, I enjoyed working in my vegetable garden in my backyard. I raised tomatoes, peppers, and cucumbers.

Lynn Is Born

On July 10, 1954, Mary Ann gave birth to our first child, Lynn Anne. She weighed a slight four pounds, eleven ounces. After she was delivered, a rash was evident on the inside of both of her arms. She was given penicillin to heal an undefined infection. We became frightened for her life because she had a very serious reaction to penicillin and developed areas of rash over her legs and her body. She began to lose weight. In a day or two, because there was no improvement in her condition, she was moved to Children's Hospital.

Pediatricians and skin specialists were baffled. Different medications were given to her and applied to the rash areas. Lynn continued to lose weight, falling to only about four pounds. The outlook was not good. We were informed that due to her condition, her body was not receiving nutritional benefits from her feeding. We were worried for her life. I prayed for her improvement.

One of the physicians thought that perhaps her condition could be improved if she was wrapped in gauze with medicine from head to toe. It appeared to me to be a last resort to cure her condition. Therefore, a medicinal ointment was applied to the gauze and was used to cover every part of the body from her toes to the top of her head including most of her face. She remained covered for two days.

On the third day, the doctor informed us that the infections and eruptions on her body appeared to be drying up. Within a week, her skin looked substantially improved and the gauze was removed. Her stomach area showed the largest eruptions.

We were told that these eruptions would be cleared up eventually, but might be visible in her belly area when she was wearing a bathing suit. I thought to myself, "Thank God. She will live." I wasn't really worried about her belly area. The rest of her turned out to be fine except for some eruptions on her legs that eventually disappeared as the years went on. At this time, I was more concerned about her health and her weight loss. We took Lynn home. She improved, gained weight, and, in due course, this matter became history and her health remained in good condition. I still feel a deep sense of gratitude toward Milwaukee Children Hospital and their staff for saving Lynn's life.

In October 1956, Mary Ann suspected that she was pregnant again. We knew that our apartment wouldn't be large enough to accommodate a second child. The following April, I discussed with Mary Ann that I would look for a new flat with more room. We found and rented a place that we liked. It was the lower floor of a two-story brick house located at 1974 South Thirteenth Street. It had a kitchen, dinning room, living room, and three bedrooms. We were pleased. It was only one block away from Allstate. I liked the idea of living very close to work in case I would be needed at home with the birth of our second child in June. We rented out our now vacant apartment on West Kilbourn Avenue for added income.

Randy Is Born

Randy was born on June 19, 1957. I had to rush Mary Ann to the hospital because she was having heavy labor pains. We arrived at the hospital and didn't have a moment left to check in or wait. We took an elevator immediately to the second floor. She was rushed to the labor and delivery room down the hall. I sat down in the waiting room. There was another young man sitting nearby about three chairs away. I took a deep breath, picked up a magazine and began to glance at its pages.

A physician came out with a baby in his arms and called out. I looked at the man waiting there and thought, "Is he deaf or what? He's not responding." He didn't budge a bit.

The doctor called out again. As soon as I heard his call again, I thought, "That's me!" I jumped up over to him.

He said, "Sam, you have a baby son." I was thrilled to death. I looked his body over and saw everything was all right. Everything looked in order, and he didn't have any rashes or skin infections. I couldn't believe how quickly Mary Ann had delivered our son; it seemed like no more than ten or fifteen minutes. We had agreed to call our baby Randal if a boy. When Randal was older, at his request, we called him Randy. I now was the proud father of a son. I gave out cigars to coworkers and friends.

My Involvement in Professional Associations

After I returned from New York and before I moved to Milwaukee, I renewed my friendships with buddies I knew before the war and who were now back home. Most of these men were attending a college or university under the GI Bill of Rights. Wally Bauer, Tom Mills, Bob Denton, John Robertsen, Caesar Banks, Frank Clark, and I decided to form a club. We agreed upon the name as the Order of the Kinsmen, to signify a close connection with each other.

Wally asked me to be president. I argued with Wally that he should be the president because I was the only person in the group who wasn't attending college. I recall Wally or John Robertsen saying that he and others were studying business and other related subjects by attending classes and studying textbooks that did not compare with my experience with the business world in New York City. I appreciated this compliment and felt a sense of satisfaction that my friends admired me for having the guts to start a business in New York City of all places.

I felt honored to be become president of our new club. Our meetings were held at Ogae Thompson's restaurant in Kenosha, a popular and pleasant dining place on the corner of Twenty-third Avenue and Sixtieth Street, now known as Bombay Louie's. We started with twenty-five members. We held a few meetings and enjoyed our camaraderie and discussions. But slowly, our membership number began to dwindle. Members were leaving town for occupational or educational reasons, upcoming marriages, and for other reasons affecting their future. Our meetings became shorter.

Eventually, the club was dissolved, but we kept in touch with one another. Years later, sometime in the 1980s, we had a grand reunion at a tavern and hall owned by Frank Clark and his wife, Ruth, in Jefferson, Wisconsin, a little ways west of Milwaukee. I was a close friend of Frank starting back before the war. They did a wonderful act to arrange such a memorable reunion.

Then in 1956, after I had been working for Allstate about three years, I joined an investment club to broaden my knowledge about stock investments on the New York Stock Exchange. An investment club normally consisted of five to twelve members. A club could have more members, but if it reached a certain maximum number specified by the Securities and Exchange Commission (SEC), then the club would be subject to compliance with SEC's operating and reporting procedures. To avoid these reporting procedures, most clubs kept their membership small.

Purposes, goals, and objectives for each club varied. A club could be organized primarily for social reasons, or for wild and speculative investment reasons, or for safe and secure investment goals, or for investments in growth stocks only, and so forth. Our club was a serious investment club with a primary goal of studying, analyzing, and selecting growth stocks.

Normally, during these meetings, members would take turns providing their analysis and recommendations for purchasing stocks to match the club's investment objectives. Members would invest their money toward the purchases of shares as decided upon and recorded in each member' account. We would regularly review our portfolio's investments.

Ed Werner, the leader in our club, and I would meet at times and share a couple of beers at a nearby tavern. In one of our discussions, he explained his thoughts that we should start an Investment Club Association in Milwaukee. We thought it would be a good idea due to the large number of investment clubs in our area. We contacted people we knew from a couple of other clubs. I tried to convince Ed that I thought he should be the president of the association and I the vice president. He instead urged me to serve as the president and master of ceremonies at the meetings, with him as vice president. I accepted. We held our election at our first board meeting and all who volunteered were nominated and elected.

We had eight hundred people at our first meeting to listen to club officers' reports and investment experts. I introduced our main speaker, a professor from Marquette University, and shared his prestigious credentials and his worthy contributions to the investment world. When he took the podium, he said, "Thanks Sam, for your fine introduction. That's kind of you. I don't deserve all that. I'll do all I can, not to disappoint all of you." I don't recall the details of his speech but recall he did not disappoint us and received a tremendous applause after his speech. I recall our members listened to and respected his views regarding investment goals and objectives of great interest to investment club members.

We had good meetings and became involved with activities of the other clubs. I met and made friends with many interesting individuals.

Chapter 15: Our Years in Ohio

During my first four years with Allstate, we sold only automobile and homeowners insurance. Then, in 1957 to 1958, Allstate began to offer life insurance to the public, so I began to sell life insurance. I enjoyed this added challenge and made many night calls to increase my commission income. I became one of the leaders in the sale of life insurance for Allstate in Milwaukee. I also enjoyed Allstate's out-of-town conferences for agents and their wives that provided sumptuous dinners and gala celebrations. It was a great company to work for!

My Brother Vince-Joins the Prudential Insurance Company

My brother Vince had his first job with the Simmons Company in Kenosha. Simmons manufactured the popular Beautyrest mattress. In the early 1950s, he was the youngest Simmons foreman. He was a bright man, as he still is today. He was transferred from Kenosha to Columbus, Ohio. Vince would occasionally come back to Kenosha to visit us.

While working for Simmons in Columbus, he was contacted by the Nationwide Insurance Company about becoming an insurance agent. Insurance companies were reputed to have excellent recruiters. Apparently, this recruiter was successful in talking Vince into starting part time as an agent prior to a full-time position.

During this time, John Rovello, manager of the Buckeye Agency for the Prudential Insurance Company in Columbus, Ohio, contacted Vince. John was known as an outstanding recruiter and convinced Vince to leave his valuable full-time position with Simmons and his part-time position with Nationwide to become a Special Agent in the Ordinary Department of Prudential in 1956. Successful agents earned executive-type high-bracket incomes but on a commission basis only. The term "Pru" was regularly used by agents in place of Prudential.

Debit insurance agents worked in the Prudential Debit Department. These agents had their policyholders in a defined area and visited their policyholders on a weekly or monthly basis to collect policy premiums. They received a salary plus a commission. Most of their time was used to collect premiums. Some of their time was devoted to selling more life insurance to their policyholders. However, special agents did not go to homes to collect premiums. These policyholders mailed in their premiums or authorized monthly deductions from their checking account. Special Agents devoted most their time to new individual and business prospects as well as to the sale of life insurance plans to their existing clients. They earned their entire income on a commission basis only.

I Join the Pru in Mansfield, Ohio

When Vince would come to Kenosha to visit our mother and dad, Emil, me, our spouses and children, and some of his friends, would often visit with him as well. We talked about our work quite a bit. Initially, we didn't discuss whether I should consider the Prudential Insurance Company. Vince came to love the Prudential and his manager, and remained a highly dedicated employee until his retirement in about 1995. He loved "Old Mother Pru."

After Vince had worked as an agent for a while, John Rovello promoted him to division manager of the agency's detached office that was located in Mansfield, Ohio, about seventy miles south of Columbus.

In May 1958, on one of Vince's trips to Kenosha, he talked me into meeting his manager in the near future in Columbus. He said that John recognized my insurance and sales experience and would offer me an excellent salary against commissions if I would move to Ohio and become a Special Agent in his agency. I told Vince I would think about it. Vince called me again, and I agreed to meet Vince and John in Columbus. My brother had previously explained John's background, his success as an agent, and the growth of the Buckeye Agency under John's management. I looked forward to our meeting.

I left Milwaukee and went straight to Vince's house and shared time with him, his wife, Mary, and their three small daughters. At this time, Linda was six; Cathy, five; and Sharon, two. Lori was not born yet. Then Vince and I went to John's large and beautiful house in an affluent neighborhood. I met John and his gracious wife Lu. After some chitchat, John began our meeting in the early evening.

The meeting continued into the early hours of the morning. We discussed his reasons why I should leave Allstate to join the Prudential. I was impressed with John. He had great powers of persuasion and superior recruiting skills. He was of Italian origin and had served in the U.S. Armed Services in Europe during World War II. I had utmost confidence in his goals and his high interest in the men who belonged to his agency. I could easily see that my younger brother was learning from a master.

This was a big decision to consider: moving to a new city with my wife and two children, ages four and one, and depending upon life insurance sales commission earnings to support my family. I knew that the failure rate for life insurance agents in their first year was very high. Finally, at 3 a.m., I said, "OK, I'll come to Mansfield."

After a good night's rest, I returned home and informed Mary Ann that I had accepted my new job with the Pru. She was not thrilled about this move, but she understood this was my call as the sole breadwinner of our family. Most wives followed theirs husband to the cities where their husbands worked. We began making necessary arrangements for our move.

I notified Allstate and submitted my resignation. I was no longer concerned about receiving the shares of stock owed to me in my stock plan with Sears Roebuck because I had been employed by Allstate a required minimum of five years and thus had 100 percent vested interest.

I gave notice to our landlord. But I decided I would keep our income property on Kilbourn Avenue to continue to receive rental income. If needed, I could hire a rental agent to care for the property. My brother Emil lived in Kenosha, but I didn't want to burden Emil with this matter. After two years, I hired a real estate agent who sold my property while I was living in Mansfield.

Before we moved from Milwaukee, I had visited Mansfield to rent a house for my family and also visited the Buckeye Agency's office to complete necessary employment documents. After all needs were finalized, I made arrangements with a moving company. We arrived in Mansfield safe and sound and settled into our new home.

Working Long Hours for Success

In June 1958, I began my new career as a full-time life insurance salesman. After I passed the license exam for the State of Ohio, Vince began to indoctrinate me about procedures, meetings, applications, forms, etc. He also introduced me to two agents he supervised and to his secretary. I particularly remember Russ Fisher, a family man who wanted to be a successful and dedicated agent with all his heart.

I studied all the materials Vince gave me. I didn't waste a moment's time to begin prospecting and making calls. I made strictly cold calls out of the telephone book. I didn't have any friends or prospects for easy sales. I continued to work long, hard hours, making telephone calls, and keeping my daytime and evening appointments. Vince and I worked days as well as evenings after dinner at home with our families. I was not nervous about my sales ability, but I did fear the prospect of failure if I didn't sell enough insurance policies to maintain and increase my weekly paychecks. I had failed in business before. I didn't want to fail again.

I kept a large chart on my wall in front of my desk. I used one color of pins for calls, another color for prospects, another color for appointments, and another color for sales. A couple of the agents laughed at me. They sort of thought I was loony or something.

Vince and I enjoyed working together very much. We visited a short time with each other in the office every day. I recall our pleasant and challenging times when he would make calls with me each Thursday night. He made excellent presentations to my prospects and made some sales for my account. It was each of our goals to become leaders in sales rankings in our agency and the Pru. When he and I and our wives and children were together, we drove our wives crazy. We talked on and on about the insurance business.

I continued to make calls to my prospects every day except Sunday. After I received completed applications for insurance policies, I would complete the reverse side to send to our underwriters in the home office for approval and issuance of the policy. I enjoyed my work in prospecting: meeting people, explaining the benefits of our insurance plans, and recording my activities for our Friday morning conferences. I enjoyed it all, except when I needed to take time out from sales to do my paperwork.

I don't recall complaining about anything other than having to complete the "darn blasted" applications for sales I had made. When a couple of agents in our office would hear me, they would laugh, saying, "You poor man! I wish I had that problem!" Each Friday morning was spent filling out more paperwork and reports for Vince. All agents were required to complete their work reports of the week and their work plans for the next week for individual reviews with Vince.

I became a sales leader in the Buckeye Agency. My toughest competitor for the number one sales position was John Spellman, who worked out of the Lima, Ohio, office. I admired this young man. He was only twenty-one years of age, the youngest agent in our agency. He possessed outstanding sales skills and an attention-getting-voice, and showed great powers of persuasion. Spellman and I met a few times and made joint calls to observe each other's style and pick up pointers.

The Buckeye Agency had approximately forty agents, but only a handful in Mansfield. We received a bulletin each week that showed sales for all Buckeye agents. One day, Russ Fisher, an agent in our Mansfield office, confided in me that before I had arrived, he thought individual sales shown for agents outside of Mansfield were intentionally exaggerated to inspire agents to believe that they could produce the same amount of sales. He told me he was pleased to witness my volume of sales and became inspired. He complimented me and expressed his appreciation. Vince began to add more agents to his staff.

John Rovello visited Mansfield every month or two. First, he would conduct a meeting to inspire us toward higher achievements. He was a master at keeping our attention. Then, he and Vince would hold a private meeting with agents who were not doing well and needed special attention. In those days, managers didn't hesitate to censure any agent's attitudes and work habits. Sometimes, a meeting would last for two hours or more. John and Vince would set up a work schedule and demand that it be carried out. John was also a master in explaining his expectations. No one at Buckeye ever doubted he was captain of the ship.

Honored as a Million-Dollar Producer

In December 1959, I finished my first full year with the Pru, having sold one million dollars in life insurance benefits, based on face value. I was Buckeye's first million-dollar producer and the company's first million-dollar producer in the greater Mansfield area. My sales were made to individuals and business owners.

I mostly sold family plans to benefit family members and endowment plans for college or retirements purposes. Any term insurance sold was given very little credit in calculating an agent's production in sales. I was No. 37 in sales rankings in the nation for life insurance sales in Prudential's Ordinary Life Department and No. 4 for the sales of individual health insurance policies.

John held an agency meeting in Columbus to honor me. I was thrilled with receiving special honors. I could feel my heart pump against my chest when I was asked to the podium. I recall I received a standing ovation and hope that in my excitement I expressed thanks and appreciation to John and my brother Vince for all their help and guidance to help me reach this honor.

When I would speak to agents at an agency meeting, I recall I explained two principal reasons for my success: hard work and convincing sales presentations. I disclosed that I had no secrets.

I also had a very strong belief in the value of life insurance, especially for the support of widows and children in the event of the premature death of the breadwinner. The Depression era and my father's illness and death left our family without income for the necessities of life. I spoke with heartfelt conviction about the need and benefits of life insurance. I articulated my belief that ownership of life insurance is truly a profound expression of love.

In honor of my achievement, Prudential placed a congratulatory announcement with my picture in an ad, the size of one-third of a page, in the *Mansfield News Journal.* One day while I walked into a bar-restaurant with one of the other agents, the bartender said, "I saw your picture in the paper. It shows you earned one million dollars selling insurance! That's a lot of money. Congratulations!"

I replied, "Thank you, but it doesn't mean I *earned* a million dollars. I wish I had earned a million dollars. It means I sold a million dollars worth of life insurance."

He said "Oh. Congratulations anyway."

It hadn't occurred to me previously that a million-dollar producer could be viewed as having earned one million dollars rather than as having sold one million dollars. This would have been an easy way to become a millionaire.

Sunday Football: Inside or Out, Rain or Shine

Vince and I were avid football fans, as was our brother Emil back in Kenosha. We listened to games on the radio, and watched them on television as soon as they began to be televised.

Being from Wisconsin, we were Green Bay Packers fans, but Packers games were not televised in that area of Ohio in those days. We also were not able to watch the Cleveland Browns play, because neither of our landlords would allow a high TV tower antenna bolted next to their dwellings. A TV antenna at least twenty feet high was required to be able to receive TV signals from Cleveland.

While living in Mansfield, my brother and I each decided to build new houses for our families. We each purchased a lot in a new subdivision a short distance out of Mansfield. My house would be located on the top of a hill. Vince's house would be at a lower level, about two blocks away from my house. We thought there would be a possibility my home would be high enough to receive a Cleveland station without an antenna.

We hired the same building contractor. Vince and Mary would own a ranch style and Mary Ann and I would own a tri-level house. We had a lot of fun during the construction process. As soon as my house on the hill had been roughed in, I asked an electrician to install a temporary electric outlet on one of the studs in the highest middle room. He did. There was no roof yet. On the very next Sunday, we brought my TV to the house, plugged it in, and held our breath. It worked! We were able to get the Browns games each Sunday. The picture wasn't perfect, but we were in our glory. We were thrilled! These were the days of James Brown, one of the best football backs of all times.

One Sunday when it rained, we watched a game with umbrellas over our heads because my house was not yet covered with a roof. Then, after our houses were finished and antenna towers were built, we were able to watch football in the comfort of our homes. Honest to Pete, one might almost think that being able to watch football was the real motive for our new houses. Not so. We wanted nice homes for our families.

Promotion and Relocation

In 1961, my brother was transferred back to the Columbus home office as John Rovello's assistant agency manager. I was promoted to take Vince's position as division manager of the Mansfield office. I missed Vince and the family.

I was enjoying my success at work, but Mary Ann didn't like it when I would invite agents to come to our home. She was not an outgoing type of person and preferred quiet and solitude. Company executives then believed a wife played an important part in her husband's success. It was common for district sales managers to have picnics, barbecues, and dinners at home to build a bond with their agents and their wives. Most agents were married. Therefore, wives would customarily be invited and encouraged to meet with the other wives and become friends. Mary Ann did her best and cooperated.

As a division manager, I spent most of my time recruiting new agents, training new agents as well as our established agents in the Mansfield office, and supervising their sales efforts. I often made joint sales calls, especially with new agents. I attended general agency meetings in Columbus and the monthly district manager meetings with

John Rovello and Vince. I enjoyed a certain degree of success as division manager in Mansfield, but I had a much better record as an agent.

In connection with his promotion and his move back to Columbus, Vince had sold his house and earned a decent profit. Later, when we decided to sell our house and move back into the city, I was hopeful I, too, would make a decent profit on the sale of my house. First, I decided to save the sales commission by acting as my own agent rather than using a real estate company. I placed a “For Sale” sign on the property. My selling price was $25,500.

I received an offer for $25,000 the very first day my sign was up. I thought, “There must be a lot of interested folks in these homes in our subdivision. I’ll wait for my selling price.” As fate would have it, I didn’t receive any offers in response to our newspaper advertisements and open house showings for a long time. Because we hadn’t received an acceptable offer for a year or so, we decided to move into the city, where we would like it better. Therefore, we rented out our house and rented a single-family dwelling at 81 Reba Avenue in Mansfield.

Friendly neighbors and shopping were nearby. Lynn now was eight years old and Randy was five. We had a number of boys in our area ages fourteen to sixteen who played baseball quite a bit. I recruited a number of the kids, formed a team as their coach, and joined a baseball league in our town. We played regulation baseball. Three times a week, we would practice all fundamentals of baseball, such as infield and outfield movements and catching, stealing bases, sliding, and more. We had a good team but lost in the playoffs to an American Legion team.

A year later or so, a real estate agent sold our previous home after I reduced the price to $22,500. I thought, “I’ll never do that again. If I ever have a serious buyer, I’m not going to quibble over $500.” I had learned a lesson.

Heading Back to Milwaukee

In the spring of 1963, I informed my brother and John that I had decided to leave the Mansfield office and return to Milwaukee. I told Vince I wanted to spend time with some of my old friends. I recall he said to me that I could remain with the Prudential in his region and then go back home and visit my friends. But I had other reasons on my mind as well.

Except for my brother Vince and Prudential meetings and dinners, I did not have a social life in Mansfield. I knew that I could watch sporting events in Milwaukee and have a larger choice of movies. Mary Ann did not enjoy sporting events or movies. Therefore, I became accustomed to attending these events alone. I missed Milwaukee and big-city living and my friends.

I also considered that perhaps some day in the near future I would work as a general agent for a well-known insurance company and develop my own agency. My personality has always been better suited for ownership and operation of my own business than for working as an executive for an employer.

I was not sure what I would do for employment in Milwaukee, but I considered remaining an agent for Prudential. However, I wanted to wait until I returned there first.

Before I left Ohio, our region's executive director came to visit me from the Florida home office to urge me to remain with the Pru as a good candidate for a future agency manager position in South Central, one of Pru's largest regions. Despite his offer, I did not feel that this would be a suitable alternative. I wanted to return to Milwaukee. I didn't know my long-term plans, so I didn't ask for a transfer. I didn't want to use such an option unless I had made a firm commitment in my mind that I would remain with the Pru.

In my five years with Prudential, I had developed good relationships with wonderful people, including the company's field leaders and their executives. I believe their intense desire to motivate and help individuals to succeed in terms of their own personal growth and professional development offered a strong basis for memorable bonding relationships.

Most outstanding in my mind besides Vince and John Rovello were Frank Brennan, Bob Beck (who later became president of the Prudential Insurance Company), and Jack Lees. I also remember Buckeye agents such as Russ Fisher, John Spellman, Arthur Kent, and Joseph Pettite. There were many others.

Outside of Prudential, the most outstanding agent of all is Al DeSimone, agent for Equitable Life Insurance Company in Kenosha. He has served thousands of his policyholders, his church, and the community for more than a half century. I had the honor to buy my first insurance policy from him when I was eighteen.

Chapter 16: Joyous and Sorrowful Times in the 1960s

We moved back to Milwaukee in June 1963. I rented a temporary home on Thirty-seventh Street near Cherry Street. By accident, I bumped into Henry Liegler, a Kenosha friend I shared time with after the war. Hank had flown as a machine gunner on B-17s in World War II over Germany. He lived nearby with his wife, Kathy, and children.

Hank was a fine man with a subtle, yet terrific, sense of humor. I had provided help and encouragement to him to purchase a two-family dwelling. He passed away years later due to illness on October 8, 1993. Betty and I keep in touch with Kathy, who still lives in the same house. I remember Hank's humor. One of my favorites was when I would call him: I'd say, "Hank. What's new?"

He would answer in a slow way, "S a v e your m o n e e."

My other favorite was that when a pretty and shapely woman would walk by or be seen, he would say, "Uuh! I bet she can't even cook." (Most married women then cooked two or three meals every day.)

After returning, I immediately made contact with Bill Reis of the William Reis Agency, one of two Ordinary Prudential agencies in Milwaukee. I accepted a position in his agency, and remained for six months or so. His was a new start-up agency. Bill and I met every morning for many weeks and would discuss insurance sales and agency matters. He was a good man. He worked hard to build a successful agency.

Milwaukee's other agency was a well-established Prudential Agency named the Fry Agency after the agency's manager. Fry was known as a top agency in the Prudential Midwest Region. Their leading agent at the time was named Len Barian.

Our Family's Love for the Packers

My return to Milwaukee coincided with the beginning of the legendary Vince Lombardi era for the Green Bay Packers. The Packers would become one of the greatest teams of all time with one winning season after another. I watched the Packers play every game during the regular season and playoff games beginning in 1963. Since that day, I have never missed a single regular season game, watching either in person or on TV.

When I could not obtain tickets for games in Green Bay or Milwaukee, I watched the game at home. If the game was blacked out, I would travel to a city where the game was not blacked out and watch the game there, usually in a tavern. Most times, I would go with a friend. My wife Mary Ann didn't care for football. But years later, after my divorce from Mary Ann, my wife Betty, who loves the Packers, and I would leave Milwaukee when the game was blacked out and go somewhere that we could watch the game, usually Fond du Lac.

The Packers were winners in the first and second Super Bowl contests. Green Bay defeated Kansas City 35-20 on January 15, 1967, in Super Bowl I, and then defeated Oakland 33-14 in Super Bowl II, January 14, 1968. The Packers became America's No. 1 team. Their record during these glory years fostered a permanent bond between millions of fans and the Green Bay Packers.

Years later, as a present for one of my birthdays, Betty gave me a cherry wood shelf with six-inch individual statutes of the great players of those years standing in uniform next to one another. The players are Jim Taylor, Jerry Kramer, Forest Gregg, Bart Starr, Paul Hornung, Coach Vince Lombardi, Ray Nitschke, Herb Adderly, and Willie Wood.

In these glory years, my brother Emil and I watched the Packers while the wives talked and our children played. In 1965, Emil's daughter, Diane, and Lynn were eleven; Emil's son, Richard, and Randy were eight.

But this unforgettable Packers era didn't last forever. In the 1970s and the 1980s, the Packers had many losing seasons. Even so, Emil and I would watch all the games. I especially remember Emil sitting in his favorite recliner. During these losing seasons, he became the most vociferous complainer ever when players would not do well, make mistakes, drop passes, miss tackles, and on and on. I complained too, as did many of our friends who love the Packers. But he and I would always sit throughout the entire game. Every year, we said, "Wait until next year!"

Finally, in 1992, the Packers again became a winning team with quarterback Brett Favre, a future Hall of Fame player. He has been named the NFL's Most Valuable Player three times, the only player ever in professional football history to reach this achievement. The Packers played in two consecutive Super Bowl games in the 1990s. They played in Super Bowl XXX, January 26, 1997, defeating New

England 35-21 and in Super Bowl XXXI, January 25, 1998, losing to Denver 31-24.

After Emil's death, I watched all games with Betty, either at home or while visiting elsewhere. We lived in a wooded lot in New Berlin for many years. We had wood logs piled up on the side of the garage for our family room fireplace. When the Packers would lose on a Sunday, as they often did, I would be so disgusted that I would go outside and chop the logs with my long-handled ax to work off my frustrations. Betty would laugh and tell all our friends. Some laughed; others gave me their sympathy. Despite their losing years in the '70s and the '80s, we continued to watch every game. Green Bay Packers fans are known for their strong loyalties.

When the Packers began to win more often in 1992, I stopped putting the ax to my freshly-cut logs. I can thank Ron Wolf, the general manager; Mike Holmgren, the coach; Brett Favre; Reggie White, one of the greatest defensive ends of all time; and many more Packers players. They brought fans many years of great football enjoyment.

Whenever Betty and I would visit Randy and his wife, Jerri, in East Peoria, Illinois, on Sundays in the 1990s and up to 2003, we would all sit together and watch the Packers play. We shared many happy times. To the best of my knowledge, Randy and Steve have watched every game since then. Randy customarily purchased a yearly NFL TV season pass so he and Steve could tune in and watch the Packers games in their home. Green Bay Packers games were not available to them in East Peoria on standard network programs.

Family Holidays

After our return to Milwaukee in 1963, Mary Ann and I and the children resumed visiting my mother and stepfather. In 1944, they had purchased a three-acre farm on West Sixtieth Street in Kenosha, about three miles west of their previous home. My mother enjoyed working the land, sometimes with help from my stepfather, but he really didn't care much for farm work. My mother enjoyed working long hours. She also raised chickens and sold eggs. She owned a goat and drank its milk after boiling it.

Goat milk was recommended for her because she had had her colon removed years before and then reopened again later. My mother tried several times to pour some for me. I always refused. She said it was because I didn't like goats. She decided one day to try to fool me, so she poured me a glass of milk out of our usual regular milk bottle rather than from her pitcher. I took a swallow and said, "Ma! That's goat's milk! And you know it!" She laughed and said that she wanted to test me and see if I could tell the difference.

Mary Ann, Lynn, Randy, and I would visit my mother and stepfather every Sunday for a noon dinner and light meal in the late afternoon. I would watch football on their TV. Emil and Louise and their kids would come over too. Mom cooked favorite Italian dishes, a real treat for all of us. I recall that when the kids were little, they loved "pskehtti," a child's pronunciation of spaghetti. We immensely enjoyed our Sundays and many happy holidays for many years. We had a tight-knit and loving family. Other family members and friends also would visit; many people loved my mother. She would send them home with fresh eggs laid by her chickens, and fruits and vegetables from her gardens in the summertime.

Their small farm also had a small pigpen behind the apple orchard. From time to time, they raised a pig, then had it slaughtered. Once, a pig escaped from the pen. Amused, I watched my stepfather chase this pig all over the grounds. He became very angry because he couldn't grab on to the pig and hold it on to its hind legs to drag it. After several tries, in disgust and anger, he tackled the pig, wrestled it to the ground, grabbed the legs, and pulled it back to the pen. I thought he performed an extraordinary feat considering he was in his late sixties. I was amazed at his strength.

Dad Dies of a Sudden Heart Attack

My stepfather, Thomas Rotunda, died suddenly on November 6, 1964, from a heart attack. He was found slumped over on the ground at a lumberyard. He was not receiving care for any heart problems at the time. This was sad news for all of us. All of his children and their families and our family, relatives, and friends attended his funeral service at Holy Rosary Church and burial at St. George's Cemetery.

Some of his children lived out of town and asked to have a meeting in the evening regarding his estate. I conducted this meeting, held in the basement of his son Tony, who lived in Kenosha. About thirty people were there. I was familiar with my stepfather's financial state. He was a laborer all his life in Kenosha at the Nash Motor Company, later known as American Motors, and enjoyed a lifetime retirement plan. There were no further payments to anyone else after his death.

During our meeting, I explained that his group life insurance plan had automatically terminated when he reached age seventy-five. Because he had lived to age seventy-nine, he did not have any life insurance, except a small policy of one thousand dollars from the Metropolitan Insurance Company, and a small death benefit from the Italian American Society. The IA death benefit and the collection at Holy Rosary were applied toward the funeral bill. There were no other funds available.

I also explained that he and my mother jointly owned their three-acre farm and house and that my mother would automatically become the sole owner upon his death as agreed by them in writing.

I also fielded questions by his children, most of whom were middle aged or older at this time. They had assumed he had more life insurance than a thousand dollars. I informed them that their father had told me he named only one beneficiary—his grandson, Tony Rotunda Jr.—due to the policy's relatively small proceeds.

To this day, whenever I visit my mother and father's graves at St. George Cemetery, I also visit my stepfather Tom's grave about the equivalent of one block away. As was customary at that time, my mother was buried next to my natural father, Gaspare; Tom is buried next to his first wife.

Mother Dies of Heart Failure

Less than two years later, my mother, Concetta Rotunda (Ruffalo), passed away at seventy-two years of age, on March 1, 1966. She had been hospitalized at Kenosha Memorial Hospital for her heart problems. She died of acute congestive heart failure. I was not there the day of her death. I had been there the day before and returned home to Milwaukee in the evening. Her physician determined that she was doing well and could return home the next morning.

My brother Vince stayed over in Kenosha to take her home the next day. Vince and Emil returned to the hospital and were advised she would receive a transfusion as a safeguard before she returned home. Very shortly after she received her transfusion, her condition drastically deteriorated. Vince described to me that her body was heaving and she was moaning. She was fighting for her life and did not give in easily. Vince was reminded of how she fought through hardships all through her life. We all witnessed her strong will to live and survive when on the verge of death on two or three occasions during her lifetime due to her heart problems and colon cancer surgeries.

The following day, I received a telephone call at home with the saddest news of my life from my brother Emil. As soon as he began to talk to me, I knew something serious had occurred. He was on the verge of crying as he told me that Mom had passed away. Standing in the kitchen, I held onto my emotions as much as possible, and then burst out in tears while hanging up our wall phone. My children had never seen me cry before. My heart was slow to heal from her loss. It took almost a full year before I did not feel severe sadness regarding my beloved mother's death. I'm sure she went to heaven.

A large funeral was held for her at the Crossin-Prokin Funeral Home and mass was said at Holy Rosary Church. My brothers and their families and many relatives and friends came to her funeral and expressed their sorrow and condolences. She was a great loss for all of us.

We lost a loving and kind mother and grandmother who had more than her share of tragedies, hardships, and illness during her lifetime. She exemplified true courage and a strong will to live each time her life hung in the balance during her serious illnesses. We missed her so very much.

My mother didn't have a large estate, but she had scrimped and saved. At the time of her death, she owned the house and three-acre farm on West Sixtieth Street and her two-family property at 4922-22nd Avenue. She had the foresight to have a will and passed on her property values to Emil, Vince, and me. She passed one-half of her estate to Emil and one quarter each to Vince and me. She had informed us a few times in the years before her death that she wanted to leave more to Emil because he was blind in one eye and she was concerned about him in the event he lost his eyesight in his good eye. She was very thoughtful.

Both Vince and I accepted her generosity and thoughtfulness. When I received seven thousand dollars as my inheritance, I used it to build a new house for my family in New Berlin, a suburb of Milwaukee.

Getting Together with Emil and Louise

Before my mother passed away, she began to show signs of aging and didn't have the strength to handle large gatherings. Therefore, Louise, my brother Emil's wife, and her sister Mae, took over hosting the holiday celebrations. Emil had built a large attractive family room, dining area, and recreation area in his basement. The recreation area included a room with a pool table. We used his lower level for many years. The dining area in the lower level would accommodate thirty to forty people at one sitting. These were fabulous and memorable events.

Louise and Mae would start preparing and cooking for these days the night before. Louise tells me to this day that Mae did most of the work, but I don't think it's true. I saw Louise do much of this work too. They would create sumptuous, mouthwatering Italian meals consisting of at least six or seven courses, including a wide selection of appetizers or antipasto; a choice of salads; and servings of spaghetti, ravioli, chicken, beef and vegetables.

There would be at least four or five delicious, home-made Italian specialty desserts and a special cake baked by Mae. Her multi-layer cakes for these occasions are, to this day, the best cakes I have ever eaten. She also baked wedding cakes, but only for her close family members or friends. She never accepted money.

Mae passed away some years ago. Betty and I visited her several times during her illness while she was in a nursing home in Kenosha. Louise missed her sister very much after she passed away. Louise then carried on with cooking for these large gatherings. But over time, the number in attendance began to gradually dwindle due to aging, illnesses, and death, until these large gatherings were no longer held.

My Brother Emil Dies Instantly from a Heart Attack

We were fortunate to enjoy many years of memorable family get-togethers before tragedy struck again. While doing some drywall work at his friend Pete Rizzo's house in Kenosha, my brother Emil suffered a massive heart attack. He collapsed and died instantly on March 26, 1986.

Emil didn't like to take his medicine regularly. Louise thought he might have died from a heart attack because he was not taking his medicine at times. When Emil felt real good he didn't always take his heart pills. This sounded like Emil.

When his wife's sister, Mae Safago, phoned me at my office and informed me that Emil had suddenly died, I locked my office door and cried for a long time over the loss of my brother. He was 59 years old. I loved my brother dearly for all of our everlasting memories and miss him to this day. At times when I think of him, I have tears in my eyes.

A large funeral was held for him. Emil had many friends. He had lived in Kenosha all his life as a well-known employee at American Motors, and an active member of his community. His funeral was attended by at least 500 of his friends and relatives. It was one of the largest funerals I have ever attended. Emil worked first as a laborer, then as a union steward, and then a supervising foreman at American Motors for many years. All loved him. He left Louise, and his two children, Richard and Diana.

Chapter 17: Opening My Own Insurance Agency

When I returned to Milwaukee from Ohio and joined Bill Reis' Wisconsin Shores Agency, I wasn't sure I would remain with Prudential. In 1964, "Curly" Jansen, sales director of Wisconsin National Life Insurance Company, or WNL, contacted me. We met and discussed my potential employment as a general agent for WNL, which was headquartered in Oshkosh, Wisconsin.

Curly, who was about fifty-five years old, was an impressive, distinguished-looking man with white wavy hair. He was committed to the insurance industry and his company. He had a memorable way of exemplifying leadership in the management of insurance agents. For example, he would take a piece of string from his pocket, place it on the table, and say, "OK. Push the string to move it." Of course, the string would go nowhere. Then he would say, "Now pull the string." The string would move in the direction it was being pulled. He would follow up and say, "Don't push your men. Pull them with you."

He invited me to visit WNL's home office in Oshkosh, about an hour and half from Milwaukee. I met several of the senior members of the management staff as well as the president of the company. Before the day ended, Curly offered me an attractive straight salary guaranteed for three years to give me ample time to develop my new agency. I accepted the position and resigned as an agent of the Prudential.

Wisconsin National had been in business for more than a half century. Other general agents told me that Wisconsin National Life was an excellent company to work for. WNL didn't have offices nationwide and wasn't anywhere near the size of the Prudential Insurance Company. I had previously worked for two giant companies, but found my adjustment to a small company very easy. Wisconsin National offered competitive life insurance plans and provided excellent services to policyholders.

Studying to Become a Chartered Life Underwriter

At this time, I also began to study and attend university classes to become a Chartered Life Underwriter (CLU), a professional designation awarded by the American College of Life Underwriters. The CLU course is rigorous. A CLU is highly respected in the industry nationally for his or her knowledge and experience. I can perhaps best explain that a CLU designation is similar to a CPA designation in the accounting field.

I attended classes at Marquette University and at the University of Wisconsin-Milwaukee. I studied late at night and early in the morning for five consecutive years. I enjoyed many meetings with other agents each year to test one another before our final exams. I received my CLU degree in 1968.

I read each issue of my monthly *CLU Journal* magazines with great interest to keep abreast of new developments in the insurance industry and upcoming changes the operations of life insurance companies. I learned that many companies were planning to offer property and casualty insurance to their policyholders. Therefore, I began to consider adding property and casualty insurance plans through my agency. After all, I had gained some experience with this during my five years selling auto and homeowners insurance for the Allstate Insurance Company. The Prudential and Wisconsin National Life Insurance Company sold only life insurance and annuities at the time. They didn't sell any property and casualty insurance.

The more I thought about this, the better it sounded. This combination did not present a problem with Wisconsin National Life Insurance Company, because it had other general agents who already sold both property and casualty insurance as well and WNL's life insurance plans.

Going Independent

When my lease for the Wisconsin National Life office on West Wisconsin Avenue came up for renewal in 1967, I felt the time was right to make a change. I decided to establish an office suite as an independent insurance agent, representing major companies for all types of life, property, and casualty insurance. I would also represent specialty insurance companies such as Lloyds of London.

In the latter part of 1967, I rented my offices at 10950 West Forest Home Avenue in suburban Hales Corners not far from my home. A large sign with my new agency logo was placed on the building signpost. My logo included a circled frame with a large painted figure of a buffalo. Within the border of a circle around the buffalo were the words "Sam S. Ruffalo Associates" with the inscription below the buffalo that read, "Ruffalo, Just Like Buffalo." I had two life insurance agents in my agency at the time, and they both remained with my agency.

The next order of business for me was to contract with independent insurance agency companies to represent them. In the beginning, it was difficult to find an insurance company that wanted to appoint me as its agent in Milwaukee. I did not have any property and casualty policyholders yet. These companies were interested in finding established agencies to represent them, not "scratch" property and casualty agencies.

The ice finally cracked. After a couple of interviews with Frank Schultz, the area manager for Heritage Mutual Insurance Company, I was appointed as an agent for Heritage, a property and casualty company based in Sheboygan, Wisconsin. Heritage, now known as Acuity Insurance Company, considered my prior experience, my success with Allstate and Prudential, and my CLU designation as evidence that I would be a successful independent agent.

This opened the door for me to be appointed as agent by other companies such as the General Casualty Company, a well-known company in Madison; two large national companies, the Fireman's Fund and Continental Insurance Company; and then the Safeco Insurance Company. There were other well-known insurance companies I represented. I began to grow my agency and began to advertise my property and casualty services to individuals and business.

My agency continued to sell life insurance. My top agent, Ralph Kratochvil, worked solely as a life insurance agent. He was not interested in selling property and casualty insurance. He remained with me for several years as a successful and loyal agent until he decided to form his own agency, which he did with my approval. He worked hard to become a successful and well-liked agent.

Fireman's Fund wanted to obtain a good share of our area's auto business, so it offered exceptionally low rates to compete with direct writers in our area. Direct writers are allowed to represent only one company, such as Allstate, State Farm, or, in Wisconsin, American Family. Independent insurance agents may represent many different companies.

I advertised in my local area's newspapers. As a result, I began to write a large number of auto insurance policies for Fireman's Fund in 1970.

My office administrative assistant handled correspondence and telephone calls and our general records, but I needed additional help to stuff dozens of policies into envelopes and mail them out to my policyholders. I had set aside each Saturday morning for this function. For a while, I would bring my son, Randy, who was fourteen, to the office on Saturday mornings to stuff the envelopes. He came with me for several weeks, but he didn't enjoy it. Therefore, I did not force him to come to the agency office any longer.

Engaging in Community Activities

As I grew my insurance agency in Hales Corners and also served surrounding suburbs, I made many new friends. One of them was Miles Theurich. He was well known for his catering company in Hales Corners. He had an excellent reputation for catering delicious private affairs and business luncheons and dinners. In one of my conversations with Miles, we happened to discuss organizing a chamber of commerce association in Hales Corner. We were both enthused about this idea! To get started, we agreed that he would be the president of our new chamber of commerce in 1970 and I would be the next year's president. Between us, we signed up forty-five members.

We thought one of our important benefits for our members would be the offering of a group health insurance benefit. With only forty-five members, I knew it would be difficult to obtain any type of group insurance, but I would try. Try as I did, I was not able to team up with a reputable insurance company who would provide a standard group policy to guarantee the issue of policies to our members. Our group was too small for such coverage. They would only provide coverage to individual members who completed individual applications that showed evidence of their good health. Some of the members would not qualify health wise. The premiums to be paid by the members who applied were also too expensive.

I also volunteered my time to work with the American Cancer Society, where I saw the importance of good health insurance first hand. I made new friends through my volunteer work, which mostly involved contacting a lot of people by phone or in person to raise funds. On one occasion, while soliciting contributions, I talked with a woman who had cancer and who asked if I could help her to receive more care than she was receiving. I spoke with a society representative, and her complaint was quickly addressed. People with cancer expressed their appreciation for the volunteers' efforts to raise funds.

The next year, the members elected me as president of the Hales Corners Chamber of Commerce. I had two principal goals in mind.

One would be to have Mayor Maier of Milwaukee speak at one of our meetings to develop community relations and to bring some publicity to Hales Corners for new smaller business startups. I was told that Mayor Maier would never leave the city of Milwaukee to visit a suburb. I decided I would try to break the ice. His office informed me that my request would be considered. Joyously, I received a letter accepting my invitation. He appeared with his bodyguard, gave his speech about Milwaukee, received a hearty round of applause from the members, and then left.

My second goal dealt with removal and replacement of the ugly electric towers bordering the east side of the main artery, 108th Street, through Hales Corners. This street is also Highway 100, which leads to the freeway. Farther north of Hales Corners, 108th Street is also known as Lovers Lane.

I contacted the Wisconsin Electric Power Company to set up a meeting to discuss the removal of these towers and moving the power wires underground or to another location. A representative visited me at my office. He took notes and said he would get back to me. After more meetings in my office with one or two power company representatives, I was informed that the project could be accomplished at an estimated cost of two million dollars.

Our local newspaper in Hales Corners began to publicize this effort. The electric company and I had discussed removing the towers and placing the underground power lines in westward open areas away from the buildings occupied by business owners and the parking areas used in the rear of some of the buildings. Many merchants appeared enthusiastic in their support of this project. Therefore, a short preliminary survey was taken to test if citizens would favor a property tax increase to pay for removal of the towers and power lines. The ultimate conclusion was no. Citizens loved the idea, but not paying for it. Our local government representatives didn't display any enthusiasm for continued efforts due to its cost. The towers are still there. I'm often reminded about my efforts to get rid of the towers on 108th Street when I drive by these towers on my way to the freeway entrance.

I enjoyed serving my time in office and appreciated the hard work of our directors. We held our usual Christmas party near the end of my term with approximately 150 people in attendance. We all had an enjoyable time, including an excellent meeting, a fine choice of foods and drinks, and a few well-delivered short speeches.

Building My Own Office Building

One of my dreams for several years was to build and own my own office building. In February 1972, having the needed funds, I decided to build an office building in a prominent and busy area of Southwest Milwaukee County. The building would not only house my agency, but also provide income when I retired because I didn't have any kind of a formal retirement plan.

I found a lot for sale where I wanted to relocate. It was at 3380 South 108th Street in Greenfield. This lot was owned by Mr. Evans of Evans Furniture Store and was located between Evans Furniture and Nino's, a popular restaurant. The lot had 70 feet of frontage and was 240 feet deep. A few large new auto dealerships were nearby. The freeway was easily accessible at Beloit Road or National Avenue entrances. I believed that the most important element of a business' success is: "location, location, location" as is often expressed by real estate agents.

To design my building, I contacted one of the top architects in our area, Helmuth Ajango. He had designed the well-known Fireside Restaurant and Theatre in Fort Atkinson, Wisconsin, and the famous Gobbler circular landmark restaurant located along West Highway 94. He said he didn't mind that my building would be smaller than others he had designed. He gave me a rough sketch of an attractive and distinctive one-story building for my approval before he prepared formal plans for bid purposes. I was thrilled with his design. He also informed me that I could build it for twenty dollars per square foot, my maximum allowed cost back in 1972. I was pleased that I could have a renowned architect design a landmark building to fit my lot size. Its design complemented other one- and two-story business buildings nearby.

Copies of his plans were sent to several contractors in the area. When they finished preparing their bids, I met with each of them. They informed me that they could build my building, but the cost would be more like twenty-three to twenty-five dollars per square foot. I tried to negotiate a lower price with the contractors, but couldn't do so without significant changes. I called Mr. Ajango and described my efforts. He still thought it could be built for twenty dollars per square foot. To resolve the price problem I was having with these contractors, I asked him if he would draw another plan for me; I would pay him for it. He explained he wouldn't do so because as a matter of his personal policy he did not draw a second plan for a client if his first masterpiece was not acceptable, whether he was paid or not. I thought to myself, he is a true artist at heart.

Now I was disappointed, but I was determined to solve this problem. Having a tendency to be a do-it-yourselfer, I took the time to sketch my own exterior design not using his design. A different architect followed the overall plan with necessary refinements and structural components to obtain a building permit.

I decided to be my own general contractor and contacted many subcontractors for their bids. The mason contractor I liked best was Charlie, who confirmed my calculations that I could build my building for twenty dollars per square foot. He helped me considerably. He gave me excellent ideas for the exterior brickwork designs, especially on the two columns in front of my building. The building turned out to be more attractive than I expected. I completed the first floor. Later, I added more to the first floor, and added a second floor. The building looks new yet to this day.

My agency moved into my new office building in October 1972. The other available office spaces rented quickly due to the building's excellent location. My occupancy rate was excellent. I rarely had a vacancy. As rents increased, my income increased accordingly, and I prepaid my mortgage in full long before the end of the mortgage period. I had made a good investment. My total construction cost, including my later addition to the building, was $225,000; the land cost $70,000. I sold the building in 1994, at age seventy, for $650,000 paid in installments plus 8 percent financing for ten years.

My family and I lived only a mile away from my office. It didn't take me long to get home or back to the office. I have always enjoyed living near my place of work.

Elizabeth "Betty" Kaurich Comes On Board

In 1974, Mrs. Kaurich, or Betty as she preferred to be called at that time, applied for part-time position as our administrative assistant. She was forty-two, married with two children. She had not worked for the past twelve years. She hadn't had any experience in the insurance field, but had extensive previous experience as a secretary. She had stayed home as a full-time mother taking care of Mary and Mark. She wanted to work only part time while the children would be at school. Her husband, Lee, held a stable supervisory position for the Rexnord Company in Milwaukee.

During her job interview, she could detect I was hesitant to hire her because she had been out of the work force for all those years. She explained to me that she had kept up with her shorthand, taking dictation while listening to the radio or watching TV. She reminded me that she didn't live far from my office. But she also appealed to my bottom line—my salary costs. She offered to work for $4.75 an hour, $1.00 less per hour than my advertised wage rate. I hired her. As she later told me, it was more important for her to be able to get home quickly when the kids came home or if one of them became ill than it was for her to make more money.

A short time after Betty began her employment, she asked if she could be absent one day. She explained that she had an appointment that day with an attorney to discuss a divorce action against her husband. I was a strong advocate against divorce due to my upbringing and my Catholicism. Without knowing anything about her reasons for divorce or discussing her personal life, I encouraged her to try to work it out with her husband. She canceled the appointment and came into work.

Betty worked in my office for three years. She enjoyed her work and her conversations with our clients and other employees. She made friends easily and created a pleasant and cheerful atmosphere in our office environment. My other employees liked Betty a lot. Betty finally decided to divorce her husband, and the divorce became final in January 1977.

Unfortunately, my agency didn't have the employee group insurance or retirement income plans that Betty now needed to have. Thus, Betty decided to seek employment as an executive secretary in a large company to earn a much higher income than my agency could afford to pay her, plus receive fringe benefits. The Miller Brewing Company hired her as secretary for the plant engineering manager. Later, she was promoted to secretary and administrative assistant for the plant training manager. We remained friends. I was sorry to see her leave. She was a wonderful person and had been a terrific employee. We got along very well.

Betty and I had worked well together in my insurance office. She helped me in so many ways. She assisted me with my building's tenants and helped me to manage it. Randy, who occasionally came to my office to visit, liked Betty too. I admired her too, because she had many friendly conversations with Randy. He respected her views very much.

Chapter 18: Business and Family Life in the 1970s

Just before his high school graduation in 1975, I asked Randy what he planned to do. I was hoping to hear that he would attend college as Lynn was doing. Instead, he said, "I plan to take it easy for a while. Dad, I've been going to school for twelve years and I deserve a vacation."

I could not believe what he said. I was speechless. I had never heard such a remark from Randy. I said to him, "If you aren't going to college, what do you plan to do?

He replied, "I thought I'd live at home for about a year, take it easy, and then decide what to do."

"If you stay at home, do you plan to pay room and board?" I asked.

He asked me what the amount of room and board would be and I answered, "I won't charge you the costs, but at least twenty dollars per week."

Randy became angry and loudly exclaimed, "You're trying to get rich off of me!"

I laughed. "Twenty dollars per week? That's a big joke! Twenty dollars per week doesn't cover your meals. And this amount doesn't cover all of your other expenses for living here."

"If I have to pay room and board, I might just as well live somewhere else," he said.

I said, "OK. That is up to you. It's your decision. If you want to, go ahead."

I consulted a counselor at Randy's high school and a friend of mine who had two older sons. The counselor advised me that Randy should be on his own if that was what he wanted. My friend said that if one of his sons had spoken to him that way, he would tell his son that he would not be allowed to put his feet under the dinner table. They both thought that under these circumstances it would be a good idea for Randy to live elsewhere.

Randy Leaves Home

At eighteen, Randy moved into an apartment with a male friend. Randy showed me the apartment lease, which said they would be joint leaseholders. I advised him that if his friend didn't pay the deposit or his share of the rent, Randy would be responsible for full payments.

Unfortunately, Randy had paid the full deposit and first month's rent according to the lease terms and had not received his friend's share of either. Randy didn't have the money to remain in the apartment. I advised him to ask his landlord if Randy paid for an advertisement to find a new tenant, if the landlord would then cancel his lease. His landlord agreed to do so. Fortunately, there was a huge demand for apartments then, so a tenant was quickly approved in the first week and accepted by the landlord.

Randy then moved to a small sleeping room on top of a furniture store on South Sixteenth Street near Greenfield Avenue. I worried about him constantly and almost every evening would drive to his place and walk to the top of the upstairs stairs when I did not see his car parked outside. I would check if he still lived there. His room didn't have a door.

I was pleased to see Randy came to visit me at my office regularly. He liked Betty, and conversed freely with her. I could see he enjoyed his conversations with her and they got along very well. For this reason, I asked her to join me and go bowling with Randy. Randy readily agreed. After we would bowl two or three games, we would sit at a booth, order a soda, or snacks and talk about life in general and Randy's interests. Randy was thinking about starting a store to sell records; however, it did not materialize. I recall that there was conversation about having enough money to do so. We bowled together on several Saturdays. I enjoyed these conversations very much.

Meanwhile, I had introduced Betty to the game of golf during the noon hour. She truly enjoyed it and took golf lessons at the YMCA in Hales Corners. I also coached her at a nearby practice range while we practiced together. She learned to love the game of golf and loves golf to this day.

I continued to grow my insurance agency and serve my clients. I had good office employees and three good agents who worked for me. We represented some of the finest insurance companies that worked only with independent agents. I also provided income tax services to my insurance clients and the public during the tax season. I personally approved all tax returns prepared by my accountant.

My Divorce and Remarriage

Lynn had married and Randy had left home to be on his own. I had stayed with Mary Ann all these years because of the children. But now, they were grown up and were no longer living in our household.

I had finally made up my mind to file for a divorce. I began my divorce action in 1977; a divorce was finally granted in Fbruary 1979.

Betty and I Get Married

During my separation and after my divorce, Betty and I played golf and went out to dinner and the theater. We enjoyed each other's companionship, and our friendship grew into love. We married on September 8, 1979. At this time, Lynn was twenty-five and Randy twenty-two. Betty's two children, Mark and Mary, were nineteen and fifteen respectively.

Betty and I were both Catholics. But due to our divorces, we weren't allowed to marry in a Catholic church. Our ceremony was held at Unity West Church in Wauwatosa, Wisconsin, a suburb of Milwaukee. Our bridal party consisted of Lynn, Randy, Mary, and Mark. We held our wedding reception and dinner at the VFW Center on North Prospect Avenue. All went very well, except that the baker delivered our beautiful wedding cake somewhere else by mistake. The same baker had delivered a substitute cake for us. It was not a beautiful cake anywhere near what we originally ordered. Under these circumstances, we had no choice but to take it. Betty was so disappointed. Otherwise, our wedding was a great success. We had a fine dinner and drinks. Most everyone danced all night to the band's music.

We had rented a room for one night at the Playboy Club, a lush resort in Lake Geneva, Wisconsin, not far from Milwaukee, for the first night of our honeymoon. As a honeymoon present, the club graciously gave us their most lavishly furnished suite on their top floor at regular room rates. Betty and I were thrilled.

The day after our wedding, I had my first kidney stone attack. That morning, I had talked Betty into watching a Green Bay Packers game at a tavern and renting a room at a Holiday Inn in Lake Geneva. She agreed, and we both watched the Packers play as always. After the game ended, we entered our motel room about 4:00 p.m. I lay down on the bed just to relax and rest—nothing else. While relaxing, my left side below the rib cage began to hurt. I thought it was a temporary gas pain. It continue to be painful and then very painful. The pain didn't go away.

As I continued to have excruciating pains, I turned very pale. Betty was standing at my bedside crying. She thought I was having a heart attack. She called Lynn, who ought to know what to do as a nurse. Lynn told her to call an ambulance immediately. Betty did. She also called Randy who lived in Milwaukee at the time to tell him I was going to the emergency room. Betty was told to follow the ambulance with our car to the hospital. I remained in the emergency room for at least two hours. I begged for pain relief. The nurse told me they had to check me for a heart attack before any medication could be prescribed. After x-rays, they discovered I had a kidney stone. Lynn and Randy came quickly to visit me and bid me best wishes to be well as soon as possible. After two days, the kidney stone had passed and I was released. Betty and I returned home. This was our honeymoon.

The next day, I visited the baker who had not delivered the right wedding cake. I asked for a refund of 50 percent. He didn't want to give me any refund! I said to him, "If you don't give me a refund because you delivered a crummy cake for our wedding, I'm going to let every customer who walks into your store hear me complain about not receiving the cake we ordered and how you do business!" He gave me the refund I asked for.

Beginning in September 1979, after we moved into our newly built home in New Berlin, Betty and I attended Holy Apostles Catholic Church for almost twenty years. Then we moved to Hartland in 1997 and attended St. Clare's for five years, followed by Sacred Hearts in Franklin and St. Matthias in Greenfield.

We attended Holy Apostles masses, but not as members of the church or as parishioners allowed to take communion. If a Catholic person divorces and remarries, he or she cannot take communion unless annulments are granted. But we went to Holy Apostles anyway. Betty and I had discussed annulments of our prior marriages on two or three occasions but we decided against it. We both questioned that if we did annul our marriages, which produced children, were we not also annulling the fact that we had children by a marriage?

About ten years after our marriage, a priest recommended that we should each separately meet with another priest who served as a Catholic counselor and discuss our personal feelings about this matter. After we had our private sessions, Betty and I decided to each have our marriages annulled due to our counselor's full explanation that annulments would not affect our religious status as parents. Our priest at Holy Apostles remarried us in the church.

Two Golf Addicts

Betty and I golfed three or four times every week at Rainbow Springs in Mukwonago, about a half hour from our home in New Berlin. We also golfed at other golf courses and would always include golf on all of our vacations.

In 1995, we became members of the Westmoor Country Club, in Brookfield, close to Milwaukee. We then began to golf at Westmoor regularly. I think Westmoor is the finest country club in greater metropolitan Milwaukee; the club's dining room and dinners, especially for major holidays, are the best available in the area.

In 1997, we sold our home in New Berlin and built a new home in Bristlecone Pines, an affluent golf community in Hartland, Wisconsin. Our new home was built near the green of the third hole. Our love of golf was our sole reason for building there. Otherwise, we preferred living in a Milwaukee suburb. We continued to keep our membership and golf at Westmoor for a while, but after a few years, we canceled our membership at Westmoor because we now golfed regularly at Bristlecone Pines. Bristlecone is a long course and expertly maintained. While we lived there, we enjoyed our association with the many fine folks we met playing golf and attending community activities at the clubhouse.

Then, unfortunately, Betty required a knee replacement in 2001 and was forced to stop playing golf for at least two years. I was forced to stop playing golf the next year due to three herniated discs. I did not require surgery. We haven't golfed since 2003, but hopefully we will in 2006.

In view of these circumstances, we sold our two-story house in Bristlecone Pines and built a new one-story house in Franklin, Wisconsin, to omit the need to walk up and down the stairs. The floor plan was almost identical to the first floor of our house in Bristlecone, except we added an extra bedroom. We moved to Franklin in November 2003, immediately upon the completion of our house, just in time for Christmas.

Chapter 19: About Betty

Betty was born Elizabeth Bajuk on January 10, 1932, in West Allis, Wisconsin, daughter of John and Julia Bajuk. Her mother, Julia Horvath, was born June 29, 1904 in Verivertisa, Borova Croatia, Yugoslavia, and came to America in 1922. She passed away March 4, 1973, from pneumonia. Betty's father was born November 23, 1904, and came to America in 1920. He became a U.S. citizen on February 21, 1925. He passed away June 3, 1972, due to a cancerous tumor attached to his heart.

Julia and John owned a house in West Allis until the Depression years began. They then sold their house and moved to Eighty-second Street near Greenfield Avenue in West Allis. Their first child, Rosemary, was born August 30, 1930, a year and a half before Betty was delivered by a midwife, Mrs. Kripsha.

Betty's mother divorced John in 1936. As a result, she was excommunicated from the Catholic Church. John ran away from Julia and the children to live in Chicago where he could not be forced to pay child support or alimony. Betty's mom had to be supported by the county for food and rent money. Betty's grandfather brought them fruit and vegetables in the summer months. When Rosemary was six and Betty was four, they held hands while walking to the supply depot, in rain, sleet, snow, or sunshine.

Betty's mom met Thomas "Tommy" Babich at St. Augustine's Catholic Church. They were married on February 14, 1942, so he would not be drafted to serve in World War II and could provide support for Julia and her two children. Tommy worked at the Allis Chalmers Company until he retired. He never missed a day of work but drank heavily, starting Friday night after work until 6:00 p.m. on Sunday. Then he would go to bed to sleep it off. Fortunately, while growing up, Betty and Rosemary spent their weekends with their aunts and uncles who lived nearby. In Betty's mother's later years of life, she was cared for in a nursing home. During her illness, Tommy went back to Europe. He passed away at the age of seventy-two from emphysema. He had promised Julia he would leave half of his estate to Rosemary and Betty, but didn't do so.

Leopold (Lee) Kaurich and Betty Get Married

Betty attended Jefferson and Washington grade schools, Horace Mann Junior High School, and West Allis Central High School. Lee Kaurich, her first husband, went to Boy's Technical School and graduated in 1949. Lee and Betty met when they were sixteen at a dance at St. Augustine's Catholic Church. Lee was born October 23, 1931. He was drafted into the U.S. Army in 1952. He was not assigned to Korea.

As soon as Betty graduated from high school in 1950 at age eighteen, she became employed by a large Catholic publishing company called Bruce Publishing for four years as a secretary for the manager of the order service department. Bruce Publishing occupied nine floors in a downtown Milwaukee building that has been replaced by very expensive condominiums. Then Betty went to work at Allis Chalmers. These were the days when men snapped bra straps of young ladies who walked nearby. She wouldn't stand for this kind of harassment and quit after a week. She then became employed at General Electric as executive secretary for the manager of the personnel development department.

Lee and Betty married September 25, 1954, after six years of courtship. Betty's mother thought very highly of Lee as a fine, hard-working man. After their marriage, Betty's grandfather John gave Lee and Betty the down payment needed to purchase a home.

Their first child, Mark, was born June 26, 1960 in Greenfield, Wisconsin. Their second child, Mary, was born July 31, 1964, in Milwaukee. While the family lived in Franklin, Mark and Mary attended Hales Corners Elementary, Whitnall Middle School, and Whitnall High School until they graduated. They did not attend college.

Throughout their marriage, Lee worked for the Chain Belt Company and then for Rexnord, which purchased Chain Belt. He worked as a draftsman in the engineering department.

Betty worked for General Electric for five years until 1960, when she left GE to take care of her new baby, Mark. Then, almost three years later, Mary was born. Betty stayed at home for fourteen years to take care of her children. She really wanted to have at least two more children, but her husband Lee didn't want any more children.

Her sister Rosemary married Robert "Bob" Skibinski. She gave birth to three children, Carla, Roger, and Victory. Bob should be canonized as a saint. He has survived very serious illnesses and operations and cared for his wife through many of her illnesses as well. He worked all of his life at Nordberg Manufacturing Company in Milwaukee to the date of his retirement.

Betty keeps in regular contact with her half-sister, Marion Casto, who is a wonderful person. Marion lives in Niles, Michigan. We visit Marion; her daughter, Denise Garlanger, and her husband; and Marion's grandson, Koty, who Marion adores. Marion is divorced and works at Lakeland Hospital in Niles as a phlebotomist. She also has two sons, John and Raymond Casto.

About Mary and Mark

When I hired Betty in 1974 to work part time at my insurance agency, she began her day in the office at 8:00 am and left at 3:00 pm with one half hour for lunch. I took advantage of the fact that she was very good at shorthand, and began to communicate more frequently with my employees and my clients. I was able to devote more time to other matters to grow my agency. In addition, Betty obtained an insurance license so that she could discuss binders of insurance with our agency's prospects and quote premiums for different personal lines of insurance and thereby served as an agent for me.

I remember the first time I met Betty's daughter, Mary. It was in 1975 when she was eleven. We were standing outside in front of my office building and I asked, "Mary, do you like school?"

She said, "Yes. I like school."

Wanting to converse some more with her, I commented, "You are a tall girl for your age." I don't recall her response.

I do recall the next morning when Betty came into the office, I mentioned, "Mary looks like a very nice girl."

Betty cheerfully remarked, "Yes. Thank you. But you know what Mary said to me on our way home. You are married to your office building."

You know, a small child's thoughts can have meaning to them. I thought to myself, "It's true, I do spend a lot of time in my office and overseeing the upkeep and management of my building. Mary was not very far from wrong."

After graduation from Whitnall High, Mary worked at a gift shop in Milwaukee's airport. She married Terry Sowinski and later gave birth to their son, John, who we called "Jon Man," on July 3, 1982. Mary didn't like Wisconsin weather, so they moved to San Antonio, Texas. She divorced Terry in 1984 and remained in San Antonio.

She married Richard Duran February 11, 1987. Richard, a fine family man, was born on Christmas Day, 1951. He had twin sons, Josh and Justin, from his first marriage. Richard and Mary took care of the three boys. Richard then adopted John. Mary and Richard love each other very dearly, and the boys, who are now men, love and respect Mary and Richard very much. The boys have all graduated from college. Richard has owned a successful electronic supply distributorship for many years. Mary works with him every day in his business.

Betty visits Mary, Richard, and the boys every year at Christmas time for approximately twelve days. She returns home before Christmas to be home with me so that we celebrate the holiday together. Before she leaves, she personally takes care of decorating our two interior Christmas trees, the fireplace, halls, and stairway. I hire a decorator for our exterior decorations. Richard and Mary come to our house about two or three times a year.

Betty is very close to Mary. They love each other's companionship and especially their times on the phone. They speak to each other every single day of the year at least once or twice. To save on long-distance charges, we now have the same cell phone service because there is no charge for these calls. Mary is a delightful woman, full of enthusiasm for life just like her mother.

Mark was a sports enthusiast par excellence. He loved sports such as baseball and football. He kept himself very well informed and reminded me of my brother Vince as a boy. Mark wanted to be a sports radio announcer. A short time after he graduated from Whitnall High, he attended a sports announcing school, but did not pursue any further studies or contact smaller radio stations for any announcing jobs. He immensely enjoyed being a guide for tourist companies.

Betty and Mark had a very close relationship for many years prior to and during his marriage. Betty would travel by airplane to see Mark wherever he lived in the United States, but not outside the country. I didn't go with Betty to faraway places because she likes to travel by plane, and I stay away from planes as much as possible due to my fear of flying. They had many memorable times together. When Mark came to Wisconsin, the three of us golfed together. Betty took Mark to some of the best well-known golf courses in our country. They stayed at first-class resorts. They were as close as a mother and son could be. Mark couldn't have afforded these extravagant outings, but Betty was delighted to share her time and good fortune with her son.

Mark loves to travel. As a single man, he traveled to foreign countries such as Turkey, New Zealand, and others. Then a few years after

Mary moved to San Antonio, so did Mark. He married Christie Wilcox of San Antonio on November 18, 1995. Christie had a daughter named Nicole whom Mark adopted. Their marriage ended when Mark divorced Christie. Mark moved to New Zealand and didn't keep in touch with his mother for a few years. They resumed contact after he returned to America.

In the spring of 2006, Betty decided to clean out our basement. Mark had left many of his personal belongings in our basement for many years. Before throwing them out or giving them away, she decided to contact Mark by phone. Mary had his phone number. Mark returned her call.

He asked, "Could you send me a list of what you have? I don't remember all that I left. After I receive the list, I'll let you know, what to send to me."

Betty said, "OK. After you get the list, let me know what you want. I'll pack it and send it to you. I'll give what's left to Goodwill. OK?"

He agreed. After he received her list, he called Betty and gave her the items he wanted. She packed his belongings in a couple of boxes and sent them to him. She called him by phone a week later and left a message asking him to let her know if he received the items. He called a few days later because he was out of town and informed her he had received them.

They began to speak more often by phone. Betty has been very happy to hear from her son again. He also informed her that he is now happily married to a lady from Taiwan. He and his wife contribute much of their time to volunteer efforts to help the food pantries, their church and other community activities in their town, Eugene, Oregon. Mark called Betty by phone on Mother's day to wish her a happy Mother's Day. Betty was truly delighted.

Betty and I Travel to Special Places

I personally was not one much for a lot of travel until later in my life. I felt that I had done enough traveling during World War II when I sailed to various large cities on three continents. We played a lot of golf and had traveled out of town mostly to golf courses. In 1986, one day, Betty said to me, "We hardly travel. We should go places while we are young and can go. Don't you think so?"

I said, "Well, where would you like to go?"

She replied, "How about Las Vegas? We can watch first-class famous shows, gamble a bit, and see the lights at night."

My friend Wally Bauer and his wife, also called Betty, lived in Riverside, California, about a four-hour drive from Las Vegas. We agreed to meet in Las Vegas. I made reservations at the swanky Caesar's Palace for three nights. We met there and spent two evenings with them in the casino.

While sitting in the casino, I asked Wally, "Do you visit here and gamble much?"

He informed me, "Sure, we like to gamble and come here about once a month. We make out pretty good."

I remarked, "I'm not very lucky. It's really tough to win in these places. I usually don't win anything. Betty has fun playing the slots and considers the time and money spent as entertainment. She doesn't lose much. We're not lucky."

He said, "We don't think like that. We play with a positive attitude when we play. We expect we will win and not lose. Most of the time we're ahead."

That night, we joined Wally and Betty and sat next to one another near the same slots. My wife made a remark, "These are hard machines to win on. I think they take your money too fast."

Despite our poor luck, we kept still and didn't complain any more during the rest of the evening about losing money. We are not gamblers anyway, so Betty and I didn't lose much. I always say this to my friends, "If I should win, say five hundred dollars, it won't change my lifestyle anyway. But if I lost fifty dollars, I would feel the pain more so than the joy of winning five hundred dollars. I feel the same way about the stock market. That's why I like guaranteed bonds."

We had a good time with Betty and Wally, who left the next day while we made our preparations to return home.

We have been on cruises to the Bahamas on two occasions and to Alaska once. We also have traveled to many famous places in the United States, eaten at finer restaurants, played at beautiful golf courses for many years, and had season tickets to stage plays. We go to movie theatres to watch highly rated movies, and of course, we are loyal Green Bay Packers fans.

More of Our Favorite Trips

In 1987, we attended a health care conference in Boston with Lynn and her children. We stayed at a plush new Marriott Hotel and all enjoyed our times together visiting the sights. We had a delightful time up until the day before we left. I had been outside the hotel for a short time. As I walked back into their huge front lobby with their beautiful marble floors, I noticed a large crowd of people formed into a circle looking on. I walked up to the crowd and took a look. I gasped for air when I saw Betty was lying on the floor in agony. I nervously rushed to where she was laying on the floor.

"What happened, Honey?" I asked.

She answered, "I slipped on the floor in a puddle of water. They have called an ambulance." So we waited, fifteen minutes, thirty minutes and then, finally, after an hour wait, an ambulance arrived from the rear of the hotel. I was fuming that it had taken so long. Betty was brought to Boston's Women's Hospital. After she was released with crutches, we returned to the hotel. I asked the manager why it took so long to get an ambulance. He explained that as a policy, they do not have an ambulance come through the front of the hotel. They use the alleyway to the rear of the hotel, which sometimes takes a long time to navigate.

I thought, phooey with them. I won't ever go to that place again. In order to ambulate, Betty used a wheelchair. We headed back home by plane. An airline employee took care of getting Betty on and off the airplane in a wheelchair.

One of our most memorable trips was a trip to the Bahamas in 1986, hosted by the General Casualty Insurance Company, one of the companies my insurance agency represented. As their guests, we stayed in a first-class hotel on the famous Paradise Island.

On another cherished adventure, Betty and I drove to and from Yellowstone National Park. I drove up and down the narrow, winding, single-lane one-way road very carefully. Anyone who has been there will vouch that extreme caution and attention is required on the narrow roads through the mountains. For many miles, there were no walls or fences of any kind or any side roads. All that was visible from the car's side window was thousand-foot drops. How often I said to Betty, "You would think they would add something to these roads in case the driver turns his steering wheel a bit off the road. Then it's good-bye."

I recall she often said to me, "Just keep your eyes on the road."

We stayed at a lodge in Yellowstone for one night. We visited Old Faithful, a wondrous geyser, and hot springs. We walked to some of the many scenic views. We had excellent weather.

Betty and I agree our most spectacular trip to date, never to be forgotten, was our tour on the new Crown Princess to Alaska—an awesome and super scenic adventure. We enjoyed an excellent stateroom with a balcony overlooking the water.

Our trip began with us headed for Anchorage. One morning, when Betty opened the shades, she called out to me, "Sam, come here!"

I came to the window and there, very near our ship, was a most beautiful glacier. We both exclaimed "What a beautiful sight!" Glaciers combined with mountains present the most scenic sight on earth. And being so close to a glacier, and its extraordinary surrounding scenery, provided us with a life-long memory of nature's miracles.

After we arrived at Anchorage, we took a domed train ride through Denali Park. We expected to see grizzly bear, moose, and wolves on the way, but we didn't see them. We did see sheep and caribou. We were most fortunate indeed because the weather was clear. Therefore, we could see the most spectacular sight on our continent, Mount McKinley, huge, awesome, and majestic with its snowcaps on a sunny day in July. We were able to see its top from many miles away. We stayed at a lodge overnight. The next day, we took an all-day bus tour of Denali Park to continue to witness its beauty.

We proceeded to Fairbanks the following day. Its restaurants served the best-tasting salmon I had ever tasted. We also learned interesting information at the Sled Dog Racing Grounds and museum.

Our most recent trip, a romantic one, came in September 2005 when we drove through Michigan into Canada to the Canadian side of Niagara Falls. We stayed at the Marriott for three nights in a room with a full view overlooking Niagara Falls.

After the porter dropped off the luggage in our room, Betty and I stood there in amazement. I said, "I was here many years ago on the American side, but I didn't ever see a view like this. It's awesome."

She remarked, "I would just like to sit here and take this all in. It's gorgeous!"

I said, "OK, but not for too long. Let's find out what are their special tours we should sign up for."

We saw many Niagara Falls attractions. The "Maid of The Mist" boat tour took us in front of the American Falls and then into the basin of the Canadian Horseshoe Falls. What a thrill! We were very close to the bottom of the falls, nearly underneath the exhilarating power of thousands of gallons of falling water. Then, we rode to the top of the Skylon Tower to the observation deck, visited and played at the Niagara Fallsview Casino, and visited the Imax Theatre, Canada One Factory, Botanical Gardens, Hershey's Chocolate Factory, and several boutique shops. We left early Monday morning and drove home on the American side taking U.S. highways. We had immensely enjoyed every moment.

My Wonderful and Loving Wife

I love my wife very much. We share each other's full-time companionship in sickness or in good health, for better or for worse. She has a wonderful personality. We have been married for twenty-six years. We are both Catholic and remarried each other in the Catholic Church about ten years ago after we annulled our prior marriages. We attend church each Sunday.

We have many common interests, such as golf, and enjoy most activities together, except for her sewing and my computer activities. Unfortunately, she finds it difficult to do activities that involve brisk or lengthy walks because she has had a knee replacement and problems with her other knee. But she doesn't let much slow her down, we still enjoy limited travel, visits with friends and relatives, and many other pastimes. We especially enjoy sharing time with our friends while eating out and enjoying an evening's conversation with them about old times and our memories.

Betty and I have not missed a dinner out together for our birthdays or our anniversary since we married. Our anniversary is September 8. Betty has this date on her license plate. If someone asks her, "What does September 8 stand for?" she answers, "It's our anniversary, so my husband won't forget it."

For each special occasion and holiday, we buy each other a card expressing our love. We read the cards to each other and hug.

I very much appreciate the many things she does for me in our day-to-day lives, such as cleaning up my mess after I cook one of my special favorite dishes. I usually cook more than one meal at a time and freeze them. She also keeps the house in neat condition with a helper on Thursdays. She enjoys gardening and caring for our flowers and bushes. She loves birds and keeps our outside bird feeders near our patio filled to the brim.

And most of all, I am thankful for our love, if one of us is ill or unable to walk or drive, we take care of and help each other as a first priority day or night.

Betty and I married September 8, 1979

We couldn't resist tasting our wedding cake.

(L-R) Louise and Emil, Godmother Luigina Caldario, and Vince and Mary at our wedding - 1979

Lynn and Betty's son, Mark, in our bridal party - 1979

Lynn's first husband, Bob,
and their two children, Lisa (L) and Sarah,
in our back yard - 1987

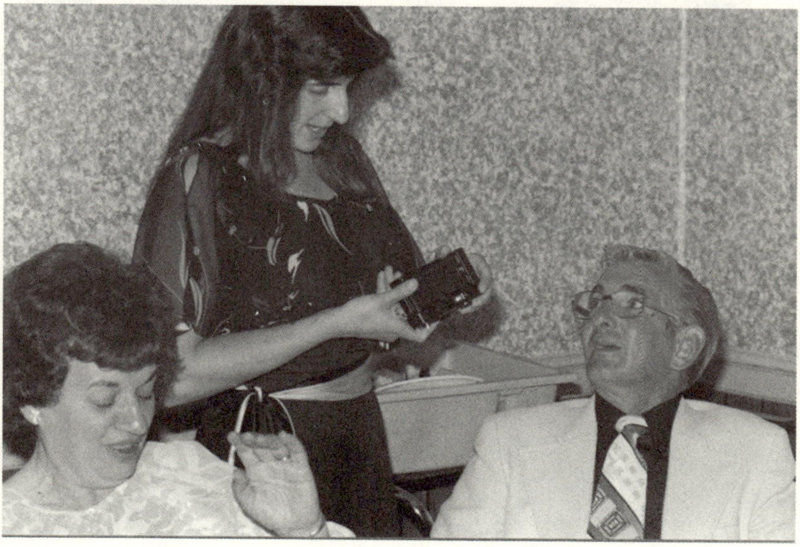

Louise and Emil with their daughter, Diana

My daughter, Lynn, in our new house at Christmas - 1979

Lynn and Bob at Christmas time – 1979

My brother Vince,
father of my four lovely nieces

Lori, my niece, on her wedding day in October 1987

Lori and husband, Bill Casazza

Vince, Mary, Betty, and Me
at Lori and Bill's wedding

Linda, my niece, and husband, Bryon Dutcher

Cathy, my niece, and husband, John Callahan

Sharon, my niece, and husband, Jim Hoover

Richard and Mary at Summerfest in Milwaukee - 1993

(L-R) Betty's son, Mark, and Betty, with Richard, Mary, and their sons: Josh, John, and Justin - 1989

My four grandchildren:
(L-R) Jill, Steve, Sarah and Lisa - 1989

Grandchildren Steve and Jill,
Christmas at our house -1989

My son, Randy, and his wife, Jerri, with Jill and Steve

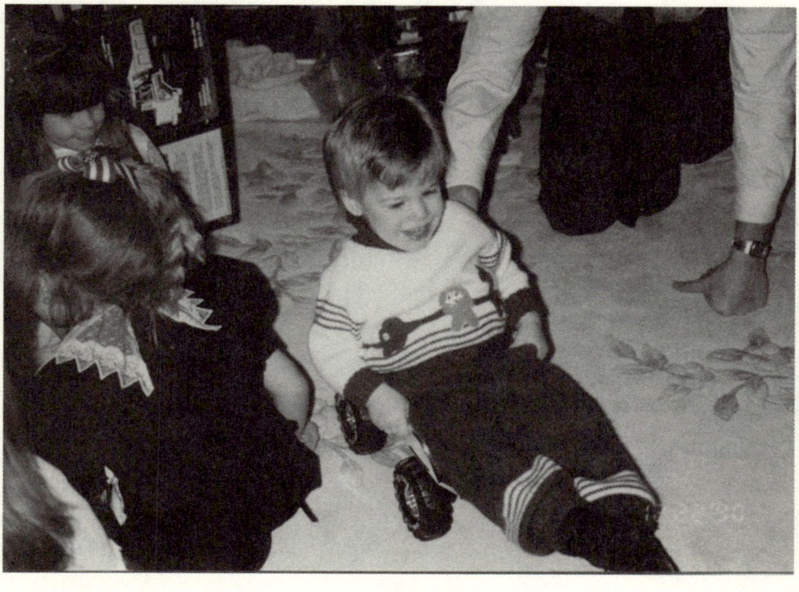

My grandson, Steve, at age 2,
taking his first ride in our living room

Family at 1991 Ruffalo Family Reunion:
Me, Tom, Lynn, Sarah, and Tom's son

(L-R) Bill and Lori, Me, and Tom and Lynn

Chapter 20: Not Time to Quit Working Yet

In 1980, after having been in the insurance field for thirty years, I thought about retiring and offering my agency to my son, Randy, not for money but as a gift, "lock, stock, and barrel." I dreamed that Randy would accept ownership and carry on the family business. My agency was well known in the southwest suburban areas of Milwaukee. I felt I could retire and continue only to manage my office building, occasionally servicing a few of my life insurance clients. Randy was twenty-three at the time. I was disappointed when he didn't accept my offer. I decided to retire anyway; therefore, I sold my agency to Hartung Insurance Agency.

I retired. But I continued to supervise my office building and also spent several months dabbling in commodities to occupy my time. I learned during this time that making money in commodities proved to be very risky. I also began to conclude I didn't really want to retire after all. My mind was on tract to get back into business. As an entrepreneur at heart since my teens, I began to again reach out for a way to be in business.

Lynn Wants to Change Her Occupation

When Lynn was twenty-six years old, she and her husband, Bob Jaeger, had their first child, Sarah, on September 29, 1980. I became a proud grandfather for the first time.

We were having lunch at a restaurant in February 1981 when Lynn told me that she was thinking about leaving her nursing job at Milwaukee Children's Hospital to become an interior decorator.

I said, "Lynn, interior decorating is a tough business in which to make a living. It's mainly a commission business. Unless you would have wealthy clients who needed a decorator, you would starve to death. You are earning a good salary at Children's Hospital. It could be a long time before you would earn such income."

While we continued to talk about her desire to leave Children's Hospital, I had an idea. At the time, my office building had a vacant space of nine hundred square feet on the first floor. I thought that this space could be used to establish a business to utilize Lynn's skills as a nurse.

I remembered that Lynn had worked as a temporary nursing assistant in a nursing home near our house while she attended class at the Milwaukee Extension of the University of Wisconsin. One day, Lynn had brought me to the nursing home and introduced me to her patients there. Lynn was always proud of me as her father. I enjoyed meeting her patients. Lynn went on to earn a bachelor's degree in nursing.

We discussed her experience and education as a nurse and how she could use these skills in establishing a business for temporary nursing services. I asked her, "Lynn do you think that even though your experience is in a children's hospital, you would be able to hire and supervise staffing nurses for hospitals and nursing homes who work primarily with adults?"

She answered, "Sure I could. I know what nurses have to do to care for patients. It won't be a problem."

Lynn expressed confidence that she would be able to assemble tests to be used for assessing the skills of registered nurses, licensed practical nurses, and nursing assistants, as part of employment procedures. (Soon thereafter, nursing assistants became certified nursing assistants.) She also felt confident that she would be able to discuss nursing skills with hospitals and nursing homes.

I also asked her, "How would you feel about calling on hospitals and nursing homes to sell them our services? Do you think this will be difficult for you?"

She answered, "It's not a problem for me. I could do it. I'm not afraid of calling on people."

We discussed how she would visit with schedulers at healthcare facilities to market our services.

I decided to invest in a start-up nurse-staffing agency. I was willing to invest all necessary funds needed. Lynn would take care of nursing functions, and I would be responsible for forms and records, employment laws, payroll, budgets, insurance coverage, and company administration based upon my prior experience. I was glad I had begun to learn about computer business programs during their infancy in 1980 and 1981.

In the beginning, we referred to our agency as a supplemental staffing agency, more commonly used then, rather than as a temporary staffing agency. There would be no rent to pay in my office building until there would be sufficient earnings. I would furnish working capital as needed. Lynn and Bob did not have any money to invest in a business.

I suggested to Lynn, and she agreed, that she should continue her job at Children's Hospital on a full-time basis, and work in my new company part time until there would be sufficient earnings to pay her the same salary she earned at the hospital. I would not draw any salary for myself until there would be sufficient profits.

Lynn and Bob had recently purchased a home. Lynn liked the idea of working part time at the temporary nurse staffing business and continuing to work full time at Children's Hospital to see if the business would succeed. I was overjoyed with the thought that I could be working with my daughter. I was confident due to my many years of experience in business, my advisory status to many business folks, and my education that I could manage a staffing business that would be very similar to an insurance agency except for the type of service offered.

In my opinion, ownership and operation of a temporary staffing agency is quite similar to ownership and operation of an insurance agency. I had been in agency business for thirty years. The major difference was in the type of services offered. I had real confidence in Lynn's knowledge as a nurse to handle the qualifications of our temporary employees. The similarities follow:

Insurance Agency:

- An insurance agency provides protection for financial losses due to unexpected occurrences.
- An insurance agency's principal objective is to sell and service insurance policies to individuals and businesses. An insurance agency recruits and hires office personnel to perform office duties connected with the sales and services to the agency's clients. An insurance agency recruits and hires agents to obtain and service clients.

Staffing Agency:

- A staffing agency provides nurses to avoid unneeded and unexpected suffering for patients in healthcare facilities due to lack of adequate nursing services.
- A nurse staffing agency's principal objective is to sell nursing care services to hospitals, nursing homes, and other healthcare providers. A nursing agency recruits and hires office personnel to perform office duties connected with the sales and services to the agency's clients. A staffing agency recruits and hires a marketing

person to obtain and service clients. A nursing agency recruits and hires nurses to provide nursing care services to its clients.

Lynn and I got along very well and she had a wonderful personality for sales. More than once, as I observed Lynn's sales efforts in the first few months, I was impressed with her techniques, especially over the telephone. I marveled at her ability to do well in her sales approaches over the phone, and conjectured she must have been listening to me make my insurance sales solicitations from home while she was growing up.

As father and daughter, our business relationship was based on much more than a handshake. I always knew with all my heart I would treat her more than fairly, with her interest uppermost in my mind. Lynn did not ever question my views or my advice and had complete trust in me. Shortly after the company began, I informed her that upon my death, my testamentary trust contained provisions giving her full and sole ownership of the agency.

NurseCall Corporation Begins Operations

I filed an amendment with the Wisconsin secretary of state to change the name of my corporation from Sam S. Ruffalo Associates Inc. to Nursepower Inc. I moved in some furniture that I already owned and purchased additional furniture for our reception office and the clerical office. We were ready now to advertise, recruit nurses, sell services, and schedule shifts with hospitals and nursing homes.

I entered into a help-wanted advertising contract with the *Milwaukee Journal Sentinel* and immediately placed ads for registered nurses, licensed practical nurses, and nursing assistants. I had used the *Journal* for classified and other advertising for many years. The day after our first ad appeared, I received a letter from Manpower, the largest staffing company in the country. Manpower's legal department advised me that it would commence a lawsuit if we did not immediately discontinue the use of Nursepower in the conduct of our business, saying the name was an infringement on its trade name rights.

Of course, my legal counsel recommended that I not get into a legal battle with Manpower, but instead choose a different trade name. Lynn, Bob, and I agreed on the name NurseCall. Bob had artistic talents, but he didn't care to be an artist for hire. He gracefully drew up a logo idea I suggested. He did an excellent job. I registered it as a trademark in our state and then later registered the logo as a national trademark. Our trademark pictured the drawing of silhouetted nurse in uniform with her nurse cap within a circle.

We needed a scheduler as soon as possible to greet applicants and visitors when Lynn would not be in the office. We hired an experienced scheduler named Karen on a part-time basis. She had previously worked for Upjohn, a well-known and reputable health company also engaged in temporary nurse staffing services. Gradually, Karen's telephone activities calling hospitals and nursing homes for shift orders began to pay off. She received her first orders from hospitals. Lynn was also involved in these activities. She began contacting a few of her RN friends, and hired two or three of them part time to take shifts.

I began to teach her business fundamentals because she didn't have any such knowledge. I felt that if anything happened to me, she would need to know about business organizations. I explained the differences between a sole proprietorship, a partnership, and a corporation; the advantages and disadvantages of each, and other business subjects. Eventually, I also informed her about corporate board of director meetings and corporate bylaws.

I wanted to be helpful to Lynn and Bob. During Lynn's employment with NurseCall, Bob was laid off, and I gave him a thousand dollars to start his own mobile shoe retail business. Bob had sold shoes in a retail store, and thought he could succeed using a van to sell shoes. I didn't get involved in his business because I didn't have time. He seemed to enjoy it, but he did not turn a profit and quit after three months. Later, he obtained a job as a machine operator, then became an electrician for the Wisconsin Electric Power Company and subsequently was promoted to supervisor. Bob and I got along very well.

The Need for Money to Expand

Each Friday, Lynn wrote out two, three or four payroll checks to our first employees. During the first several weeks, NurseCall didn't have funds in its checkbook to pay our part-time office schedulers, and Lynn would come to my office upstairs each Thursday. I would give her a check out of my personal checkbook payable to NurseCall to cover these wages plus expense payments due. Under tax rules, we were allowed to wait until the end of the month to send in withholding and Social Security taxes to the Internal Revenue Service and Wisconsin's Department of Revenue. Later, when our payroll became larger, we paid withholdings and Social Security taxes each week as required.

NurseCall began to show signs of increasing shift orders from a few of our local hospitals due to existing nursing shortages. We began to grow. I began to spend much more time in the NurseCall office, so I moved my office downstairs. I rented out my office upstairs, helping to pay for NurseCall's free rent downstairs.

Due to increasing sales and potential profits, after three or four months of operation, Lynn decided to leave her position with Children's Hospital. She continued to receive the same weekly salary as she earned at Children's Hospital as I had promised.

We advertised weekly for registered nurses, licensed practical nurses, and nursing assistants in all of our local papers. Lynn visited facilities to market our services and obtain shift orders, interviewed RNs, and supervised scheduling. I continued to be responsible for management of the company, cash control, accounting, payroll reports, advertising, and overall office procedures. I hired a part-time office assistant to assist with billings, time slips, payroll, and other accounting duties. Lynn worked full time five days per week and sometimes in the evenings from her home over the telephone. I worked full time during the day at the office as well as hours in the evenings and Saturdays in the office or at home. I could do so because my children were adults now and on their own. I was indeed proud of Lynn's efforts and proud of how attentively she took great care of her new baby—my first grandchild, Sarah.

Some evenings, after Lynn would put Sarah to bed, we would speak over the phone. We discussed such matters as forecasts of shift orders, rates for our services, hourly wage rates, and gross profit projections per hour for services rendered according to nursing skill services rendered, otherwise referred to as disciplines. I would also discuss projections with her referring to my forecast spreadsheets.

Lynn was beginning to learn the importance of planning and analysis. I virtually served as Lynn's mentor at this time and for approximately ten years.

NurseCall's needs for working capital began to increase rapidly. My personal funds on hand were not sufficient to cover operating costs any longer. An infusion of new capital was needed. NurseCall did not have an approved credit rating to be able to borrow funds. I obtained a second personal loan of $40,000 from the State Bank of Hales Corners using my mortgage on my office building. (Using the 2005 Consumer Price Index, this amount today equals $86,000.) One of the reasons more capital was needed now was that our clients were waiting too long to pay their invoices. I began taking aggressive measures to visit our clients in person to start collecting our past-due accounts receivables.

We had many past-due accounts in 1981 and 1982. Interest rates were very high. The U.S. Department of Treasury reported that interest rates skyrocketed. The highest rates occurred from 17.74 percent in April 1981 to 18.35 percent interest by December 31, 1981.

What does this high interest rate have to do with collecting accounts receivables on a timely basis? It's all about money. It is the money earned on money that is due to others after checks have been written and have not yet cleared the bank. Finance officers will withhold payments or checks due during periods of high interest rates to earn interest on their money. One practice is to have the checks issued but not to mail them for a while. The period of time from the date the check is sent to the payee and the payee deposits this check into his or her account and it clears the bank as a charge against the payer's account, is referred to as the float. NurseCall patiently waited until we received our payments beyond their past due dates.

There was no point to charging our clients a late payment fee or interest charge, because healthcare institutions simply didn't pay these charges. If we forced a client to pay such charges, we would almost certainly lose the client. To improve our collection efforts, we began to telephone those facilities we served, reminding them of payments due.

The year 1981 was a favorable year not only for NurseCall, but also for most nurse-staffing agencies nationwide. In my efforts to use all the working capital possible to grow our business, I did not pay myself or take any salary or personal expenses out of NurseCall. Lynn was paid every week to help support her family.

Unfortunately, we received a sharp setback in early 1982. The unexpected happened. Due to changes in government regulations affecting payments to hospitals for benefits received by Medicare patients, suddenly we no longer were receiving orders for shifts from any of our hospitals or nursing home clients.

The Social Security Amendments of 1983 (Public Law 98-21) established a prospective payment system for hospital inpatient services for Medicare patients. Under this act, a hospital would be reimbursed according to treatment received by a patient prior to discharge, classed according to a particular procedure or type of care as defined in a Diagnosis Related Group (DRG). For example, if an appendectomy was performed on a Medicare beneficiary, the hospital would receive a predetermined fixed payment according to the classification in DRGs. In most cases, these reimbursements would be lower than prior reimbursements for the same procedures.

Hospitals could no longer expect reimbursements would be based upon inpatient days in the hospital and operating costs. Their payments would be reduced. The purpose for the establishment of DRGs was said to be to encourage hospitals to reduce their costs for care. In future years, prospective system payments became mandated for other types of healthcare services and other types of medical care facilities. Staffing agency services such as ours were seriously affected.

Due to such conditions, beginning in February 1982, we did not receive a single order for any more nurses from a hospital or nursing home. Our business came to a standstill. Orders for our services did not stop only in Wisconsin but nationwide for all agencies, to the best of my knowledge. Nurse staffing agencies closed their offices. The outlook for an early turnaround was very poor. I had a decision to make regarding our future.

Chapter 21: Providing Healthcare in Different Ways

Either we would quit business or find a replacement business and use our existing setup. I discussed this matter with Lynn and decided to investigate the startup of a Medicare-certified home health agency to provide care to elderly patients. If we were approved by Medicare, I knew my company would not be allowed to earn a single cent in profits because a Medicare agency is a nonprofit entity. But at least Lynn and I would receive salaries.

Following our investigation and understanding about the operations and costs for Medicare and Medicaid agencies in Wisconsin, we decided to apply for approval. We filled out many application forms. I would manage all affairs of the company as president and executive director. Lynn would supervise nursing functions and patient care services as vice president and director of nursing. I would continue to provide all of the working capital for operational costs and hope Medicare would reimburse me.

Relying upon my knowledge of accounting practices, I studied long hours to become familiar with federal Medicare and Wisconsin's Medicaid rules governing operations, reimbursements received from the government, and allowable expenses in order to manage my agency on a sound fiscal basis to avoid personal financial losses. Lynn studied and became familiar with approved nursing services and patient records.

I learned that if we could not secure an adequate number of visits to our patients, we would not receive sufficient amounts from Medicare to cover salaries and operating costs. I decided to accept this risk with the hopes that conditions would change in the future and we could reenter the type of nurse staffing business we operated before.

Medicare did not cover any losses or unpaid debts incurred by a home health agency, and neither gains nor losses could be applied to future or prior years to obtain reimbursements. I would personally absorb these financial losses.

We always needed working capital, so I didn't take any salaries for my services so that I could afford operating costs. Of course, Lynn needed and received her paycheck every week, in order to support her family, especially at times when Bob was laid off.

I worked within the rules of the Health Care Financing Administration (HCFA) and the Blue Cross of Iowa, which served as our fiscal intermediary and provided the money. Three of their auditors from Iowa audited NurseCall's books every year. NurseCall not only provided home care nursing services, but also physical therapy, speech therapy, and occupational therapy services to its patients. Our agency's nursing department, headed by Lynn, would visit these patients and maintain all medical care records for inspection by government agencies. I maintained all financial records, and completed required financial reports and the annual cost report. I also assumed full responsibility for all contracts, financial records, and administrative and operating procedures of the company in accordance with Medicare regulations. I wrote and enforced company procedures, job descriptions for all positions, and our company's policy manual.

NurseCall received a fixed payment from Medicare for each patient visit made by our nurses and assistant nurses. For example, in 1982, we received approximately eighty dollars per visit for an RN's visit to a patient's home. A home visit by an RN lasted about thirty to forty-five minutes, including her time at the home to write out the progress notes in following doctor's orders. We received a lower amount for payments to the home health certified nursing assistant who provided services to a patient, usually during a four-hour visit. We also received Medicare payments for physical and speech therapists.

Because we were paid per visit, if our healthcare staff did not make a sufficient number of visits to pay of our costs, I personally suffered the total amount of any financial losses. Therefore, it was imperative that we would always have sufficient numbers of visits. The more visits, the more revenues we received to pay our fixed and variable costs. We all worked hard and advertised to the extent allowed for reimbursements to obtain patients. We also received patient referrals from hospitals, nursing homes, and the private sector.

In our efforts to keep agency costs as low as possible, I did not hire an outside accounting firm to prepare Nursecall's annual Medicare cost report. Instead, I utilized my experience with accounting and my study of Medicare's reimbursement regulations to maintain our books and prepare reports for three auditors who visited our office to perform annual Medicare audits. As a result of my do-it-yourself approach, my company saved approximately $20,000 per year, the normal fee charged by an experienced accounting firm to complete these comprehensive reports. I also provided financial reports as required under the State of Wisconsin's Medicaid Title 19 program for approved home health agencies.

Medicare pre-approved Lynn's annual salary for $26,000, based on her background and her job description as vice president and director of nursing. My salary was approved for $46,000, also based on my background and job description as president and chief executive officer.

Fortunately, I was able to rely upon other sources of income for my wife and me. If I had not had such income, it would have been impossible to continue with NurseCall. I continued to hope that someday in the near future there would again be a strong demand for nurse staffing at hospitals and nursing homes, offering a renewed profitable opportunity to establish a private staffing company.

Home Healthcare: About More than Just Money

At Christmas in the late '80s, as a practice, I visited five or six of our patients in their homes with my secretary or an administrative assistant to wish them a Merry Christmas. Most patients were elderly women in the last year or years of their life. I recall a ninety-year-old patient who joyously played a Christmas song on her piano. These folks smiled often and were friendly, sociable, and lovable and added a glow to the season.

Health Staff in Illinois owned a Medicare home health agency in Des Plaines, Illinois, adjacent to O'Hare International Airport. While one of my mother's best friends and a godparent in our family was ill and required home care, I promised my old friend Ed Caldario, her son, that I would see to it that *Comare* (godmother) would receive the best care possible. I made sure our most experienced nurse in our agency would be Comare's visiting nurse. During her care, I visited her at home. We conversed a while. Before I left, we hugged, and she whispered in my ear, "Sammy, pray for me that I die." She passed away on January 30, 1991. I could see that Ed and his wife, Bunny, suffered anguish at Comare's death due to a heart attack. Within two years, in 1993, Bunny passed away in Ed's arms, having suffered from cancer.

My comare's remark reminded me of my sorrow many years earlier—my father's cancer during my childhood, my mother's illnesses, and my brother Emil's death. I nurtured a deep sense of compassion for sick people and a respect and love for the old and the feeble that began in my childhood. When my home health agency was losing money, it crossed my mind several times that if my agency were forced to close, our services rendered would have been for a worthy cause.

Demand for Health Staff Nurses Explodes

In the latter part of 1987, the tide began to change for the better! The demand for supplemental nursing services began to grow. Hospitals and nursing homes were again experiencing acute shortages of nurses and certified nursing assistants. I renamed one of my former corporations Health Staff Inc. so as not to conflict with Medicare's rules applicable to NurseCall's operations. I opened a separate new office away from our NurseCall office and named a new manager for its operation.

Medicare rules mandated the need for all NurseCall's supervisory and office employees, including Lynn and me, to keep written records on the use of our time during a two-week period of each quarter for review by our fiscal intermediary auditors. Three auditors came to our office every year from Blue Cross of Iowa in Des Moines for a full week to audit our books. They examined NurseCall's books and details of all transactions to ensure we were not using Medicare funds for personal or other business reasons. We kept excellent records, and therefore passed their audits each year. Except for their refusal to pay certain disallowed expenses, I did not have any problems with federal Medicare audits. NurseCall never received any penalties.

Medicare was very strict about using its money for reimbursable expenditures. Over the years, NurseCall suffered very little with denied reimbursement for disallowed costs. In one of our later years, we did have a minor problem with our state's Title 19 auditors. However, the problem was resolved without penalty or disallowance of reimbursements. I was proud of our excellent record. Most of the time, we received reimbursements for almost all of our expenditures; if we didn't, I footed the costs. You bet I was careful!

In 1988 and in 1989, Health Staff began to show a profit. Due to a sudden large demand for staff nursing at hospitals and nursing homes, Lynn and I were in favor of closing our Medicare office. I notified Medicare and Medicaid to terminate our participation in their programs as a home health agency. Lynn was as enthusiastic about terminating our Medicare services as I was. We would again be able to devote ourselves full time to nurse staffing operations.

Health Staff grew rapidly. It opened four new offices in Milwaukee and one in Madison. I decided to open up more offices in the Midwest. In all, we opened fourteen offices.

To strike while the iron was hot, I borrowed more funds to expand our operations into other states where demands for staffing services were growing. I obtained loans for NurseCall–from our local M&I Bank, and I signed as sole guarantor to guarantee payments with my personal funds in the event of the company's default.

Rather than waste a month or two and pay large fees for a market analysis of a chosen location's potential for success, I decided instead to open each office, test it, and evaluate actual results. I would open an office in a chosen location, hire an office manager who would also serve as a scheduler until we needed one or more schedulers, test the market for three to four months, and evaluate our potential for profit. If our new location's future appeared favorable, I kept it open; if not, I closed it.

During this initial period, we learned about the amount of demand and who used supplemental staffing nurses, competitive wage structures of temporary nurses, hourly fees charged to hospitals and nursing homes by our competitors, advertising costs, our profit potential and other related factors. Such information was very helpful in allowing us to predict with reasonable accuracy whether to continue operations or to close a struggling office. I believe our time and money invested to establish a startup office in a particular geographic location for testing purposes were well spent. Our results were more accurate and saved us a substantial sum in fees for costly market analysis prior to establishment of a new office.

Given our expansion, we needed management help. I hired our first regional manager to work in southeast Wisconsin and across the border in Rockford, Illinois. He also helped Lynn to market the business in the Milwaukee area. Each manager signed an employment agreement and a non-compete agreement. All office employees throughout our company were also required to sign non-compete agreements.

I soon hired a second regional manager in Illinois to open more new offices in Illinois, Iowa, Missouri, and Indiana. We had previously opened an office in Des Plaines, Illinois. We opened and prospered with these offices: Rockford, Sterling, Peoria, Bloomington, and Crystal Lake in Illinois; the Quad Cities of Iowa and Illinois; St. Louis,

Missouri; and northern Indiana. A few other offices were opened in the Midwest and were closed because their futures weren't favorable. Regional managers reported directly to me on a daily basis by fax and required my prior approval for the hiring of any office employees.

Interestingly, our largest agency office in terms of the number of shifts placed was located in Sterling, Illinois, with a population of less than only ten thousand! An employee had suggested we open an office there. A smart move! We succeeded there beyond our expectations because there were many nursing homes in the surrounding rural areas. Also, we were blessed with a good manager and hard working office schedulers.

We held a company dinner in Sterling to honor these employees. In advance of our dinner, I asked our Sterling manager what she would like to receive for a gift at dinner in appreciation for her efforts. She asked if I would get a hundred-dollar bottle of champagne for her. I did so. She opened it at our dinner and gave everyone a share. Lynn and I attended this dinner with the regional director and a new vice president I had hired. I had hired the vice president a few days earlier to assume full responsibility for the company's marketing operations. He had national experience with a major drugstore company. My company's psychologist evaluated his qualifications and recommended him as a qualified candidate to fill this position.

After Lynn divorced Bob in May 1988, she lived alone with her two children. Lynn and I occasionally traveled together to one of our nearby offices in Illinois so she could be home in the late afternoons to take care of Sarah and Lisa. Sarah was eight years old and Lisa was three.

At times, Lynn traveled alone to our Rockford office and our Madison office to discuss nursing services and any problems with the office manager. Each drive was approximately an hour to an hour and a half each way, which allowed her to be at home for the kids.

Lynn desired to obtain a master's degree in nursing, so she attended the University of Wisconsin Extension in the afternoons to do so and successfully obtained her MSN degree. She was very proud of this accomplishment and so was I.

Lynn and I began to receive increasing salaries due to increasing profits. I also began to recover all the personal loans I had made to the company, and years of unpaid past wages that were on the books owed to me for several years.

Our Wonderful Relationships

Because our company was prospering so well, I wanted again to clearly review my plans with Lynn. I explained to her again that my trust provided that she would obtain all shares and full ownership of the business upon my death. I was then sixty-five years old. Disposition of my assets at the time of my death has always been a serious concern to me. As an estate planner and advisor, I often discussed the effects of death upon a person's estate, and always strongly believed that individuals should plan for the proper distribution of their estates. I didn't perceive these conversations as rare or out of bounds for discussion with my daughter.

Lynn introduced Tom Hagen to me one day while in an elevator. Tom worked in our same building. Betty and I attended a wedding held by one of NurseCall's employees in June 1988, and Lynn and Tom attended as well.

Tom and Lynn dated each other regularly. They often visited Betty and me at our home for special holidays, where we shared time together.

Betty and I had spent a lot of time with Lynn and the children before she dated Tom. We met often during weekdays, weekends, and holidays. Lynn came to social affairs Betty and I conducted at our house. Lynn continued to be the fine daughter and an excellent employee as always. I was truly proud of my daughter, whom I loved very much. We got along very well in business and in our family life. Betty and I had frequent dinners with Lynn and the kids and visited one another regularly. When Lynn had other engagements, Betty and I enjoyed babysitting the kids.

We also had dinners out with Lynn and Tom from time to time. During our social meetings, Tom, Lynn, and I did not discuss business matters, a custom that we practiced for years. There may have been an incidental casual or general comment for a few moments but not a discussion. In about 1991, Tom moved in with Lynn. Tom had two sons who lived elsewhere.

Lynn was considered friendly and cordial by all our relatives and friends. She went out of her way to express her love and friendship. Often, Randy and his family and Lynn and her family, including her husband Bob and then later her friend Tom, would meet with us for special events.

When my brother Vince and his family would visit us from Florida, Lynn and her family would be at our house to share time together.

Lynn was always gracious toward my brothers and their families and our closest friends and their families from Kenosha and Chicago. She rarely missed any events, even if she had to come alone because the kids could not come along for one reason or another. She was also a helpful daughter in time of need. For example, one cold and snowy night, Lynn came to O'Hare International Airport in Chicago to pick up Betty and me and bring us home. If we had a social event at our house with our older friends, Lynn would come over to pay her respects. I could not have asked for a more ideal daughter.

Randy and his family lived in Peoria, Illinois. Betty and I would go to Peoria four or five times a year for birthdays, holidays, shopping, dinners, or other occasions. We also drove to Peoria to watch Steve, my grandson, play baseball. They also drove back and forth to Milwaukee. I was indeed a proud father and grandfather. No one on this earth was more important to me than my Betty, my children, and their children. They were the center of my life. I believe we had excellent and heartfelt family love.

Chapter 22: The Estrangements Begin

In the latter part of 1990, I organized a new temporary staffing company, Health Staff Health Professionals Inc. (HSHCP), as a subsidiary of NurseCall Inc. I appointed Lynn to operate this office and offered her a very attractive compensation plan, including a base salary and almost all of the company's profits after taxes. I wanted her to remain with the company.

She had served NurseCall as a loyal employee in the 1980s. She would now work only for HSHCP. I rented an office at 11084 West National Avenue in West Allis because it was located near Lynn's home. I kept my office in our home office at 2514 South 102nd Street, also in West Allis, until its lease expired in the end of 1992.

Lynn was given full responsibility to manage this office. She would approve employee time slips, calculate wages, pay bills out of the company checkbook, make bank deposits, and use Paychex to issue company payroll checks and pay payroll taxes. Payroll checks carried my automatic imprinted signature to save my time signing them.

Lynn kept all HSHCP records in office. I used these records to prepare monthly profit and loss statements and review them with Lynn. I kept an experienced full-time accountant on my staff to assist me. I only used an outside firm to prepare annual corporate tax returns using the financial statements I prepared.

All records were kept in our computers. I personally designed all the menus and screens for keeping and printing all of our company's accounting records. I began doing so in the 1980s, using DOS. Then Windows 3.0, 3.1, and Windows 95 came onto the scene in later years. To this day, I still have a DOS computer that contains the company accounting records and backups for 1989 through 1996. I had developed an excellent knowledge of DOS and enjoyed working with DOS. My computer programs included Word Perfect, a word program; Quattro Pro for spreadsheet reports; and, my favorite, Paradox, a powerful database program that I used for keeping our accounting records.

In 1992, after studying three or four physician recruiting firms and their successful operation and interviewing experienced recruiters to work for me, I began a new company called Physicians Group Inc. It was a separate department in my home office that recruited and placed physicians in long-term assignments at hospitals located throughout the United States. I hired two experienced representatives. They spent their days contacting hundreds of physicians in different specialties to recruit them, usually for six-month assignments at well-known hospitals. Fees for our services approximated twenty thousand dollars per physician placement. We placed only two physicians in 1992, but had favorable prospects for a much higher number of placements in 1993. Then, as fate would have it, physician placements began to suffer in 1993. Two Milwaukee companies and my company were forced to close our offices.

The home office lease expired in 1993. I did not renew it and instead moved to smaller offices at 9330 West Lincoln Avenue in West Allis. Lynn was doing well with her office on West National Avenue. I would visit Lynn's office once or twice per month and continued to prepare monthly accounting statements based upon her records. I continued to manage my office and the Bloomington office.

Competition from Tom and TopTechs

In 1992, during a luncheon, Lynn had informed me that Tom had resigned his sales position traveling back and forth to Madison selling ads for the yellow pages. She said he had organized a new business named TopTechs Temporaries to sell technical temporary staffing services to industries and businesses in Milwaukee. She told me that he had opened his office at 2100 North Mayfair Road in Wauwatosa, a suburb of Milwaukee. I really didn't take an interest in his business or become concerned. I had enough to do with management of my own companies. Further, she said he was not competing with my type of business.

In the later part of 1992, a nurse applicant mentioned during his interview that he had also recently applied for a nursing position with a company called TopTechs. Astonished, I said, "TopTechs?"

He said, "Yes. They're a nursing agency just like you are. Don't you know who your competitors are?"

As soon as possible, I contacted Lynn and asked her about this matter. She assured me Tom was not competing with HSHCP. She explained that he was doing very little nursing business with a couple of small nursing homes in Madison, in an area where we had previously decided not to do business, and not to worry.

Lynn had always been very honest and straightforward with me since the day she was born. I believed my daughter. I didn't question her any further or investigate the matter.

1994: More Gifts, and a Job for Randy

In 1994, I gave Lynn and her two children company stock as gifts, valued up to the maximum ten thousand dollars per recipient allowed under federal gift tax laws. My company's value was estimated to be near two hundred thousand dollars at the time. Under estate rules, if Lynn inherited the company upon my death, she would not have to pay any gift taxes. If she inherited and sold the company for the same value as established on the date of my death, she would not need to pay any capital gain taxes either.

Health Staff Illinois, located in Bloomington, was much smaller than the Milwaukee office. As I aged, I took fewer trips there to supervise the manager. I depended upon my local manager there to do a good job and manage it properly.

In August 1995, my son, Randy, an insurance agent for twelve or thirteen years, decided he and his wife would now accept my offer for part-time positions with Health Staff in Illinois. Therefore, he opened an office in Peoria and managed the Bloomington office. Sales gradually began to increase. They followed my instructions and did very well. They enjoyed their work and their part-time income.

I was delighted to be able to work with my son and daughter-in-law because I had more reasons to speak with them and visit them more often than I had previously. I felt our business connection brought an interesting facet to our relationship.

1995: The Relationship with Lynn Changes

In early 1995, Lynn began to complain about office procedures, the design of our billing invoices, and our computer program used to prepare invoices. In the entire time we had worked together, she had never once complained or expressed concern about these procedures. She normally took care of nursing functions in the company and oversaw nursing employee duties. I was confounded. She said, "Dad, I think we should change our invoices to a different type of invoice. And I think it would be a good idea to change our computer program we use for our scheduling forms."

I replied, "I don't understand. Our invoices have been fine-tuned and have worked very well for us at all our offices in the past. I think it's one of the most attractive designs I've seen when compared to those used by our competitors. Let's stay with it and avoid spending money for a new design. We also have a good supply on hand. In regards to our computer program, you know I've looked at many of them offered by software companies. Our program has worked out very well. It's quick and easy to learn."

Well, Lynn didn't usually argue the point and didn't comment much on this subject.

Our system was simple and accurate. Also, our part-time billing clerk who worked out of her home would not need to learn a new program. I had personally considered the purchase of different agency programs in the past, but I didn't see they were any better than our system. Another reason was that the purchase of a new program would require unnecessary costs. There really wasn't a single good reason to make a change.

I was puzzled by Lynn's complaints. I imagined that she was anxious about her upcoming marriage to Tom.

Lynn and Tom's Wedding

Lynn and Tom were married on April 8, 1995, in a religious ceremony. I walked my daughter down the aisle up to the altar and presented her to Tom. Lynn's mother was in the front row, and Betty and I sat in the next row. Lynn looked absolutely beautiful in her white wedding gown.

Many of our relatives and friends from the Milwaukee and Chicago areas, Kenosha, and other Wisconsin towns came to the wedding ceremony and dinner reception. The reception was held at the well-known Wisconsin Club on 900 West Wisconsin Avenue in Milwaukee. Tom and Lynn hired a large band.

Mary Ann, who was living in East Peoria, Illinois, and I didn't speak a word to each other. A few of Mary Ann's friends were there. Randy, Jerri, and their two children, Jill and Steve, were also there from East Peoria. Jerri looked beautiful in her dress.

Among those relatives and longtime friends who attended were my sister-in-law Louise, wife of my deceased brother Emil, and her son Richard from Kenosha; my brother Vince and his wife from Florida; Sam and Adeline Caldario from Chicago; Ed Caldario from Chicago; and Kathy Liegler and her son. We also met Tom's family members and friends.

Betty and I danced together a few times. We always enjoyed dancing. I was seventy and Betty was sixty-three, but neither of us had knee or back problems then.

Before Lynn and Tom left for their honeymoon, they brought Sarah and Lisa over to our house for Betty and me to take care of them. As usual, we had a great time with the kids for the next several days. I especially had fun with Sarah and Lisa on my computer. I had installed several games for them to play. One was a favorite program that provided the words and music for popular children's songs. We sang these songs together, as we had done before, as the words popped up on the monitor. They enjoyed it. They laughed at Grandpa's singing.

During Lynn's and Tom's absence, I took Sarah and Lisa to school and picked them up after their classes. Lynn had asked me many times in the past to bring the kids to school or to pick them up. When the girls were younger, Betty and I took them to Chuck E. Cheese's, a popular place for children, to use their play equipment. The children were very accustomed to being in our care. We enjoyed one another's company, and shared so many wonderful years together.

The Trouble Begins

Tom and Lynn returned from their honeymoon and came to our house to pick up Sarah and Lisa. The next day, April 16, now stamped in my memory as one of the saddest days of my life, I discovered that Tom and Lynn had planned a new business strategy to go with their new marriage, a strategy that didn't include me.

I stopped over at their house. Tom let me in. I walked into the kitchen. Lynn was standing at the other end near her sink.

I said "Hi, Lynn."

She did not greet me but said, "I want you to know that I've changed the locks and keys on the front door to the office. And I don't want you to come there anymore!" she said.

I thought my heart stopped. My entire nervous system was stunned. I felt suddenly weak and tried not to show my shock as I held on to the kitchen counter for support.

I replied, "Lynn, what do you mean? What are you doing? You don't have the right to close me out of the office. It's my company! I'm president and owner of Health Staff!"

I was so devastated and hurt because Lynn had never spoken to me this way. Tom went upstairs. Then she remained silent and didn't speak any more. I left the house.

That Monday, I contacted a locksmith I had used in prior years. He replaced the lock for me. I gave Lynn a new key when she came into the office. I did not fire her. I was distraught about her behavior and hoped dearly for reconciliation and my Lynn back.

In the days following our confrontation, Lynn continued to come to work at HSHCP and to perform her duties and supervising our office employees on a regular basis. But she would not speak with me. Again, I thought I did not want to fire her. I wanted to avoid losing ties with my daughter. She was a very important part of my life. I prayed her behavior and her actions would blow over and we would be on friendly terms again. I had hopes too that she would contact my relatives and friends and discuss her feeling with any of them. I recall that my brother Vince was looking forward to an explanation from Lynn but never received any correspondence or telephone calls from her. I kept in contact with my friends and relatives as always and know that she never communicated with my family's relations or my closest friends ever again. I kept up my hopes she would start to communicate with me to discuss the source of this problem and resolve it. My heart was heavy with sadness, and I hoped for the best. She continued to serve as manager and receive her full salary.

On one occasion when I stopped into the office for one of my rare visits, she did speak to me, warning that if I did not leave the office, she would call the police.

I replied, "Lynn, if you call the police I will tell them I'm your father, and owner of this company. You will look very stupid!" She did not call the police. Our office employees, with whom I rarely spoke, were within earshot of this short argument. I left shortly thereafter.

I did not have any written employment agreement or covenant-not-to-compete agreement with Lynn. Because she was my daughter and a benefactor of my estate to gain full ownership of the company, I didn't think I needed written agreements with her.

Lynn was very familiar with such agreements, as we required them of all employees, with the exception of staff nurses. She helped enforce these rules. She had participated in lawsuits against employees who violated their agreements. Lynn and I had only verbal agreements regarding her employment. In the state of Wisconsin, verbal agreements between employers and employees are not typically deemed enforceable, because Wisconsin is an at-will employment state. In general, this means an employer is allowed to terminate an employee, and an employee may resign at will. However, legal advice is always appropriate in these matters.

Upon reflection, I should have treated Lynn's relationship with the company as that of an employee. Had I done so, I feel that my loving relationship with my daughter would not have been placed at such serious risk of total estrangement.

I tried several times to meet with Lynn in late April and early May, but she would not talk with me. In a final effort to meet with her, I called a meeting of the Health Staff board of directors; the directors were my wife, and I, and Lynn. I sent her a written formal notice announcing the place and time of our meeting. She did not respond or show up. I rescheduled another meeting and notified her, with the same results. Therefore, in accordance with our corporate bylaws, I notified Lynn her status as a director and vice president was terminated immediately. She was not terminated from her position as manager of HSHCP. I chose to wait for future developments with hopes we would be together again.

Reconciliation Efforts Fail

In the middle of May 1995, Lynn asked if I would visit a counselor with her. I agreed and recommended that we visit with our company's psychologist. He had evaluated each of us in 1990 in an all-day session, finding we were each qualified for our respective positions. He later evaluated other applicants I would send to him as I filled important positions within my company. He was regarded as one of top one hundred business psychologists in the nation. Lynn and I both agreed to meet with him.

Our counselor asked me to send him a letter with background about Lynn and me prior to our first meeting. I faxed a five-page letter to him the morning of May 22, 1995. My letter described our responsibilities and our working relationship with each other from 1981 to the present.

I also included some financial information. My letter included the following statements:

> During the period from 1981 to 1988, Lynn actually received more wages than I did, inasmuch as I had income from other sources and placed top priority on her family's income needs. In 1985, I tried to obtain financing from the Small Business Admini-

> stration (SBA), but was denied. I continued to operate NurseCall anyway. So that I would be able to receive larger rental value for my office space in the Ruffalo Building (under the Medicare program), NurseCall moved to another location.
>
> I continued to loan funds to the corporation regularly for working capital. In addition, I also had to borrow funds on behalf of NurseCall from time to time to meet cash needs of the company. To obtain these loans, I had to pledge my personal assets to guarantee payment to the bank. NurseCall never defaulted in payment of its loans. In 1985, NurseCall Inc. owed me $130,000 for past wages due and personal loans I made to the Corporation, not including the bank loans I had guaranteed.

Lynn and I met at our counselor's office for two conferences, on May 22 and 23, 1995. While she and I waited in the lobby for each session, we sat away from each other and did not speak. During meetings with our counselor, we did not speak to each other either. Each meeting lasted about two hours. Lynn didn't express any conflicts that I can recall. I complained that I felt our communications had seriously deteriorated. I do recall the psychologist asked us questions about our business operations and our relationship with each other and our understanding of our duties. I don't believe he asked many questions about our goals or our complaints.

At the end of our second conference, I clearly recall our counselor recommended that Lynn and I meet alone. He said, "Both of you appear perfectly capable of resolving your own problems. You should meet together as soon as possible and bring an agenda to your meeting for discussion."

Therefore, Lynn and I agreed to meet each other on May 26 in a restaurant two stores down from our office. I carefully prepared my agenda and looked forward to our meeting with high hopes. We met in the morning as agreed. With Lynn's permission, I spoke first. I barely had spoken two or three words and she interrupted me.

She said, "Let's get to the bottom line." I really thought she was referring to the company's financial bottom line. It was not the case.

I asked, "What do you mean by the bottom line?"

She answered, "Who is going to be owner of the company?"

I replied, "As you know, Lynn, I'm already passing on stock to you for ownership in the company, as I did last year, but I will remain as the majority stockholder, until a future time."

Without a moment's thought, she abruptly stated, "In that case, I'm resigning right now."

I asked her if she would give me at least two weeks notice so I could replace her. She refused. As discoveries later showed, she had no intention to remain with HSHCP. She had already planned to leave the company to pursue her own company's goals. Lynn had different ideas about her future and no longer wanted to wait to own my company. She wanted to own her own companies. Lynn had received an excellent guaranteed salary, even in lean times, plus almost all of the net profits of HSHCP for her years of employment.

When I entered the office later that day, her employees were not there. After checking their names in the payroll records, I contacted each of them. But not one of them agreed to return to work. Therefore, Betty came to my office to help me take care of our client calls, employee calls, and visitors.

Shortly after Lynn resigned, I informed my closest friends and relatives of her resignation. They expressed their sadness with Lynn's decision. I also notified Randy and Jerri about Lynn's resignation during a planned visit. They did not approve of Lynn's actions. The emotional pain of Lynn's resignation, and her and her family's total estrangement from Betty and me and all of our relatives (except Randy and his family) and friends on my side of the family, continues to this day.

Chapter 23: Saving My Company

Lynn was gone. Our office staff was gone. I called Betty, who came to the office immediately. She had never worked in one of our nursing agencies, and didn't know how things were run, but her prior office experience proved invaluable. Betty answered phones and returned calls to hospitals or nursing homes that called to order shifts, change hours, cancel shifts, etc.

I would stand right next to Betty as she spoke on the phone with one ear and listened to me with the other. I coached her on what to say using brief, quickly written notes. She purposely spoke slowly and repeated some of our clients' sentences to inform me of the conversation so I could tell her what to say. It worked out very well. Betty did a marvelous job.

I didn't speak much with our client schedulers because, in my experience, they preferred to speak with female schedulers. I think I sounded too officious for normal chitchat. They always asked to speak to Betty. She has a much nicer voice and did an excellent job. However, I did speak to and interview applicants in our office. I also printed the various report forms we used, and prepared schedule forms and the other paperwork in our office.

I continued to work in the office with Betty during the daytime and at home in the evenings to keep my company afloat. I hired two office schedulers and a nighttime and weekend scheduler. I used the training manuals I had written for the company several years ago to teach these new employees. They began to learn how to use our daily scheduling forms, obtain orders from our clients, and fill our shift orders.

To replace Lynn as director of nursing, I hired Beverly Felton, RN, one of Wisconsin's leading nurse practitioners. She was attending the University of Chicago to obtain her medical degree. She specialized in geriatrics. I'm extremely grateful to her for all her help during that turbulent time. My last contact with Doctor Felton dealt with medical problems for one of my close elderly relatives.

In an unexpected move, Lynn's companies, Nursing Centers Inc. and TopTechs, began to contact our nursing staff at their homes. In order to recruit our employees, they offered higher wages. Of course,

Lynn knew our wage rates very well. Therefore, we offered higher wages than Lynn and Tom offered. Many of our employees eventually returned to HSHCP. We all worked hard, but my company suffered severe losses in 1995.

Disheartened by Lynn's actions, I took a step I felt was necessary to save my company; I consulted with my attorney regarding a possible lawsuit. His findings, derived from records in the State of Wisconsin's corporate division, were as follows:

Lynn had organized a new corporation in Wisconsin, named Medical Staffing Associates Inc., as filed by the state as far back as September 9, 1991. Then Lynn changed the name to TopTechs Temporaries Inc., as filed by the state on April 27, 1992. Lynn had informed me in 1992 that Tom had started a company called TopTechs as a technical temporary staffing company. She had never mentioned Medical Staffing Associates Inc. to me. Apparently she had an excellent reason to change her company's name.

Then, about a year later, records showed that Lynn organized a second corporation on February 9, 1993, as a home health agency named Nursing Centers Inc. As filed by the state on November 11, 1993, it was later changed to a temp service business. Nursing Centers was not a part of or in any way affiliated with HSHCP. In 1993, Lynn had vaguely mentioned she was going to obtain a home health agency license. I assumed she meant HSHCP should start a home health agency business again. I reminded her that we both previously agreed to close our home health agency in 1989, after nearly ten years of operation, and told her there would be no purpose for us to have a home health agency again. As previously stated, our home health agency operated as a non-profit entity to earn salaries. A noticeable demand for staffing nurses did not exist.

The above mentioned corporate registrations and annual reports are available as public information from the State of Wisconsin's Department of Financial Institutions' corporate division.[4]

Legal Action Begins

My attorney and I decided to start a lawsuit to protect and save my company. I also hoped that I would be able to open the door to communications with Lynn and Tom during this process. Pretrial proceedings bring the parties together at the conference table and can be used to open up discussions. I had high hopes for positive and

[4] Further information is available at www.wdfi.org/apps/cris/.

meaningful discussions because I had had almost no contact with Lynn, and none with Tom and my grandchildren since Lynn and Tom became married, despite my personal efforts to communicate with them. I was frustrated with this rift because there had never been any prior family disagreements, hostile acts, or arguments involving Lynn, Tom, or the children, ever.

To the best of my recollection Lynn had never expressed unhappiness with her position in the company verbally or otherwise. During a brief conversation 1990, I recall she expressed her interest to run her own office. Subsequently, I formed Health Staff Health Care Professionals as a subsidiary of my parent company, NurseCall, and placed her in charge of the office as previously stated.

I offered Lynn an extremely attractive arrangement whereby she would receive her yearly salary plus almost all of HSHCP's profits as a bonus based on each year's prior profits after accounts receivables were collected from our clients.

As sole manager of HSHCP's office, she received a sizeable base salary from 1991 to June 1995. In addition, starting in 1992, she was offered the incentive bonus of 75 percent of the calculated prior year's profits, during each subsequent year, after moneys would be collected, for as long as she remained in HSHCP's employ. She was also furnished a company luxury car. Thus, she received approximately 85-90 percent of all net profits, paid in 1992, 1993, and 1994; and she received a salary but not her incentive bonus in 1995. The company lost money in 1995.

I wanted more than anything else to have meetings together in a conference room with Lynn and Tom, Betty, and I, working toward reconciliation. Further, throughout the proceedings prior to a trial, I was determined to offer attractive arrangements to Lynn and Tom so we could be together in business, as I knew I was getting close to full retirement.

There are two principal facets of a lawsuit. Normally, proceedings prior to a trial are heard at a conference table. Witnesses are interrogated during depositions to obtain information regarding complaints, and their answers are filed. During such conferences, there can be successful efforts to reconcile difference among plaintiffs and defendants.

My attorney filed a lawsuit two and one half months after Lynn and Tom returned from their honeymoon on April 15, when they closed the door to Betty and me.

On June 30, 1995, my attorney John Clark of Miller Simon and Maier, filed a complaint in Milwaukee County Circuit Court. NurseCall Inc., a Wisconsin corporation, was named as the plaintiff, and Lynn Jaeger-Hagen, an individual, as the defendant, residing in Greenfield, Wisconsin.

Lynn's attorney, E. Joseph Kershek, filed an answer, affirmative defenses, and counterclaim as filed by Lynn on July 27.

Subsequently, Mr. Clark filed an amended complaint naming Tom, Lynn, TopTechs Temporaries Inc. and Nursing Centers Inc. as defendants. Then Lynn filed a third-party complaint on October 27.[5]

The documents for this case are readily available for copy or review at the Milwaukee County Courthouse. Information in this book may relate to parts of these filings; but it does not provide direct quotations from these records nor all of the claims, answers, and counterclaims as filed; nor does it include all of the claims and answers in the records. There are approximately one hundred pages regarding these legal documents stating complaints, answers, and counter claims filed by attorneys for the plaintiffs and defendants. Only Lynn's deposition was included in these papers. Other depositions that were taken from other witnesses are not included in these filed documents.

We did not have any personal meetings for reconciliation or discussion away from the conference room during our pretrial proceedings. But I did submit two separate written proposals to Lynn and Tom through my attorneys. My first proposal was rejected.

My second proposal in January 1996 was very favorable to Lynn and Tom. I promised I would continue passing stock to her, as I had done in 1994, until she owned 49 percent of the company, and then give her 100 percent full voting powers for operation of the company by changing my shares to nonvoting stock. I would continue to pass on all remaining shares to her at no cost to her until she had full ownership. I included a guaranty of the transfer to her of any remaining shares in the event of my death, thereby saving on gift taxes.

Lynn was also offered a choice to make a counterproposal for purchase of NurseCall. (It owned HSHCP.) I also stated that if this proposal was not accepted, I would sell my company in the near future.

Before my attorney submitted this, he said to me, "Sam, this is a generous proposal. Are you sure you want to do this?"

I replied, "Yes, it's what I want to do."

---

[5]The case number containing filed documents is Case No. 95CV006407.

But the proposal was rejected. I had wished very much that a lawsuit would encourage open communications at the conference table and lead to reconciliation and merger, but it didn't.

Settling the Business Differences

My history in the management of my companies demonstrated that I did not hesitate to go to trial in a lawsuit against any employee who violated company policies or agreements. In this lawsuit with my daughter, even if my case was a cinch to win, I wasn't interested in a trial because the trial would be about the Ruffalo family. The suit was not started based upon financial considerations but with forgiveness in mind and the hope of reconciliation. My efforts to work together had failed.

I did not want my family members' or my name to become publicized as part of a family feud in our community. I also felt the trial itself would increase tensions and add to our emotional sufferings.

Therefore, I instructed my attorney to offer them a very light settlement option to resolve the case: receipt of payment by NurseCall Inc. from Nursing Centers Inc., and the defendants named, for the small cash sum of $10,000 plus the return of all NurseCall's shares previously issued to Lynn or her children in her name as custodian. They accepted my settlement offer immediately.

We all signed our settlement agreement on April 17, 1996. It stated my complaints against Lynn, Tom, and her companies and her complaints against my company and me as set forth in the case. For payment received, we agreed we would mutually release and discharge each other and our successors and assigns.

The value of these gifted shares based upon my company's value according to an Internal Revenue Service (IRS) formula was estimated at $30,000. Thus, I would be receiving $40,000 in total value. But the out-of-pocket payment of $10,000 would not be hard on Lynn's pocket book. I felt confident this amount would not affect Lynn's financial ability to raise Sarah and Lisa. Sarah was now age fourteen and Lisa had reached age nine.

A stipulation and order for dismissal of the case signed by all parties was filed with the Circuit Court on April 26, 1996.

Chapter 24: Remembering the Good Times

Our family had never had occurrences or discussions of dissension, arguments with anger or temper flare-ups, drunken behavior, or any other acts of any kind causing separation or estrangements. Our times together had been harmonious and loving. Lynn and her family and Betty and I always spoke with one another in a friendly manner.

Betty and I had often met with Lynn and Tom and Sarah and Lisa for family and social affairs. There had never been a change in the frequency of our family get-togethers, dinners, baby-sitting, holiday celebrations, or hospital visits. For example, I recall that late one night, Lynn called me at home because Sarah had been brought to the emergency room at West Allis Memorial Hospital, which was very near Lynn's home. When I arrived, Tom was also there with Sarah.

The following is an overview of our times spent together prior to April 16, 1995. It indicates we didn't have family problems shortly before Lynn's marriage or in prior years. Obviously, there were business problems that I was not aware of then.

- In 1994, I gifted a timeshare interest to Lynn, Randy, and Betty, allowing rights to famous resorts throughout the world. The paper was recorded and filed as a registered deed, to pass on to them in the event of my death. Lynn had reserved a certificate to use for her and Tom's honeymoon in 1995 at Ka'eo, Princeville, Kauai, Hawaii. She and Tom later canceled this and instead made their own reservation.
- In 1994, I gave Lynn and Sarah and Lisa, with Lynn as their custodian, company stock as gifts, valued up to the maximum ten thousand dollars per donor allowed under federal gift tax laws. My company's value was estimated at nearly two hundred thousand dollars at the time. Under estate rules, if Lynn inherited the company upon my death, she would not have to pay any gift taxes. If she inherited and sold the company for the same value as established on the date of my death, she would not need to pay any capital gain taxes either. I explained to Lynn that I would transfer more shares not to exceed the annual allowed amount to avoid paying gift taxes. My computer records still contain the chart of

my planned distribution of additional shares to Lynn and her children in subsequent years.

- In 1995, before Lynn and Tom's marriage, Lynn asked me to purchase a quality diamond stone for her from my New York diamond cutter. She knew I had purchased diamonds for my insurance clients as part of their retirement plans and for investment purposes. My clients paid me a fee for these services. As Lynn requested, I ordered her choice of a high quality investment diamond stone. Of course, I didn't charge Lynn a fee.
- On the day of Lynn's marriage, I walked her up to the altar to present her to Tom. Lynn had met or shared times with many of our relatives and friends in past years and Tom had previously met them at gatherings and family reunions. All these relationships were friendly and pleasant; there was never a sign of disharmony in our family.
- Betty and I took care of Sarah and Lisa while Lynn and Tom went to Hawaii for their one-week honeymoon. If we had problems with Lynn and Tom, would they have left Sarah and Lisa with us to take care of them? I don't think so. The kids were no problem for us, and we got along with them very well.

I don't think there is a soul among all our relatives and friends who noticed any evidence that we had family problems. It's still extremely difficult to comprehend that on the day after Tom and Lynn returned from their honeymoon, Lynn broke off her relationships with Betty, me, and all relatives and friends of the family, except for my son, Randy, and his family.

Chapter 25: We Miss Them

When Lynn was two or three, I bought an 8mm camera. I made movies of our family events, vacations, holidays, and celebrations for the next thirty-five years. Hundreds of feet of film show Lynn and Randy's lives, including their grandparents in Suring and Kenosha, and spouses, children, relatives, and friends. All these films have been professionally copied to a videotape or DVD.

One of the long films about Lynn, spanning from her childhood to the next twenty years or so, and another about Randy, each titled *This Is Your Life*, were each given to Lynn and to Randy many years ago. There are many other movies in my possession, all on videotapes and DVDs. Hopefully, these films will continue to be saved and watched by my family's descendants and their children. I'm especially hopeful that Sarah, Lisa, Steve, and Jill will have them for a keepsake to enjoy in their later years.

I wanted to do all I could to reconcile with Lynn after she separated from all of us. I visited her office three times, once at Christmas in 1996, then before Easter in 1997, and then around her birthday in July 1997. Each time, she was not in the office and out of town. A receptionist asked me each time: "Do you wish to leave a message?"

I answered, "It's OK, I'll call back another time," and left. I think that most likely, the receptionist described me to Lynn. After my visit for her birthday, I received a letter from Lynn's attorney with a request not to visit there anymore. I never returned.

Wisconsin's Grandparents Association

I looked for a different means to connect with my grandchildren and Lynn, and learned about grandparent associations. For months after my and Lynn's lawsuits against each other ended, I tried to make arrangements through a social worker in Waukesha County to meet with Sarah and Lisa, but I was informed her attempts failed.

Meanwhile, I learned of other grandparents who had similar estrangements. I learned that under many state laws, grandparents are not legally able to visit their grandchildren if parents of the children object.

I joined the Wisconsin's Grandparents Association in Milwaukee and attended its monthly meetings along with approximately twenty-five other members. Ages of their grandchildren varied from small children to adults up to about 30 years of age. Each grandparent related his or her sad and heartbreaking story. Many of them were able to communicate somewhat with their sons or daughters about their grandchildren but were not allowed to visit them; others explained they were not allowed to see or visit with their grandchildren at all.

It's very difficult to believe that there are adult children who take such drastic measures to deny their parents the opportunity to visit their grandchildren. Is it a form of punishment or what?

I can easily empathize and understand other grandparents' feelings when their grandchildren are cut off from them. We shared such sadness and disappointments with one another in our meetings. These elderly people did not appear mean or irresponsible.

As a Wisconsin Medicaid home health agency as well as a Medicare agency, the Milwaukee County Department of Aging invited our staff personnel from time to time to attend their seminars about the care of people over age sixty. These seminars also included movies about the county's care programs such as senior dining sites and the delivery of meals. One movie that was shown has stayed in my mind. It showed forms of elderly abuse. The first time I saw it, I was shocked to view how adult children would unreasonably confine their non-physically disabled elderly parents to their bedrooms or misuse their parents' property or financial resources for their own selfish personal benefits. An example is cashing a parent's social security check and using it for the adult child's own purposes.

Efforts to Receive Grandparent Visitation Rights

In a last effort to receive grandparent visitation rights, I hired a lawyer. Lynn agreed to allow me to visit Sarah and Lisa one time before they left Wisconsin to live in Arizona, where Lynn and Tom had opened a new office. Lisa now was thirteen and Sarah was eighteen. It was agreed I would meet the children at McDonald's on 109th and National Avenue.

I brought a shopping bag filled with presents and placed it on the side of the booth. I had eagerly looked forward to seeing them for the first time in two or three years, and thought that perhaps I would not ever see them again due to our estrangement. I sat there and waited a short time. Lisa entered alone.

I saw that Tom was waiting for her in the car. As she sat down in the booth across from me, she said, "Sarah couldn't make it. She had to take care of something." Then she asked, "Is it OK if I tape our conversation?"

I thought to myself, "I didn't expect this." But I answered, "That's fine. You can turn it on."

I knew I didn't intend to make any negative or derogatory remarks or complain anyway. I would only have nice things to say for pleasant memories of our meeting.

Lisa turned on her tape recorder. I recall we talked about Sarah and how she and Sarah would like to live in Arizona and their attendance at school and Sarah's plans for college. My only wish for her was to have a lasting pleasant memory of her grandfather. It was important to me; I was seventy-four at the time.

We spoke for only about four or five minutes. She was anxious to go. She turned off her tape recorder, and began to leave. As she began to leave, I told her I had presents for her and Sarah, and offered to give her the bag full of presents. She refused to take them with her and left.

As soon as I returned home, I said to Betty, "Can you imagine that! Lisa asked if she could tape our conversation! Lynn and Tom should be ashamed of having Lisa do this—having a thirteen-year-old child tape her conversation with her grandfather—a terrible situation. This is not teaching them respect for seniors and grandparents."

As I though about our encounter over the next few days, I wondered, "Were Tom and Lynn worried I would lambaste Lynn and Tom, and criticize Lynn with supporting explanations of Lynn's admissions during her deposition and interrogations in our lawsuit? It was not the reason I wanted to meet with little Lisa and Sarah."

Betty tried to comfort me: "Don't let it hurt you like this. You have tried your best."

Christmas in our New Berlin home - 1993
Tom, Lynn, Steve, Lisa, Randy, and Jerri

Christmas time in our New Berlin Home - 1994
(Back) Randy, Lynn, Sarah, and Jerri
(Front) Steve, Jill, and Lisa

Lynn next to her daughters, Sarah and Lisa Jaeger,
with Jill Ruffalo, Randy's daughter,
at our New Berlin home at Christmas time - 1994

My daughter, Lynn, and Me
walking to the altar April 8, 1995 at
Ridgewood Baptist Church, Brookfield, Wisconsin

Randy, Me, Jill, Jerri, and Steve in New Berlin - 1996

My niece Linda and sister-in-law Mary in Florida

Vince and Mary at home in Ponte Vedra, Florida

Betty and Me on our 22nd wedding anniversary,
September 8, 2001, at Lake Okachee near our home

Swinging away at Peninsula Golf Course
at Fish Creek, Door County, Wisconsin – 2002

Betty ready to swing

Betty's 70th Birthday Celebration - 2002

(L-R) Karen and Keith Wiest, Albert Pitts, Ed Caldario, Bob Chiapetta, and Evelyn Pitts

(L-R) Laura Chiapetta, Evelyn Pitts, and Betty at her 70th surprise birthday party - 2002

(L-R) Tony and Lucille Maglio, Kathy Liegler and son, Gregory

My younger brother, Vince (R), and Me -
Retired Insurance Execs

Betty and Me with my Godmother
Raffaela Caldario on her 95th birthday

My sister-in-law Louise Ruffalo (L)
and her sister, Mae Safago

Betty's Class Reunion Committee (L-R): Arlene Braun, Eva Peychal, Me, Betty, Dale Voit, and Ron and Marge Gergen, at our home in Bristlecone Pines, January 2001. Earl Peychal took this photo.

Betty and her daughter, Mary, in our Bristlecone Pines home before attending the Sunset Playhouse - 2004

Alfredo Bartolini and his wife, Seglinde (Lindy)
at their Florida home - 2004

Marion Casto, Betty's sister, in her kitchen
in Niles, Michigan - 2005

Louise Ruffalo with her grandson Jerome and his wife - 2005

Louise Ruffalo with her daughter, Diana,
and her two sons, Jerome (L-R) and Jesse Dorlack - 2005

(L-R) Laura Chiapetta, Marilyn Chiappetti, Betty, Me, Marilyn's husband, Carl, and Laura's husband, Bob, enjoying a night out at dinner - 2005

Chapter 26: Time to Retire

Health Staff's name and trademark were registered with the U.S. Patent and Trademark office in 1991. In the early 1990s, I saw an advertisement: another company named Health Staff, a competitor, was operating in downtown Chicago. Our Health Staff office was west of the city in Des Plaines, Illinois.

I informed my trademark attorney in Milwaukee, who then wrote a letter to the other company about the trade name infringement. That company was based in Minnesota. In their reply, a company official stated they felt that they were not competing with us because they served the downtown area only and not our areas in western parts of Greater Chicago. I decided not to take legal action because the cost did not warrant this risk; our staff nurses didn't like to provide care to facilities in the downtown areas at night.

In early 1997, they opened an office in Madison, Wisconsin. Now they were in my backyard using my company name. My trademark attorney had retired. Therefore, I hired a new trademark attorney, who sent a letter to the other Health Staff and threatened the start of a lawsuit for infringements upon our registered rights. My attorney warned that I would either commence a lawsuit or accept payment in the amount of four hundred thousand dollars to purchase full rights to my trade name/trademark. The other company rejected my offer.

After exchanging correspondence, I decided to reduce the amount and to handle my own negotiations to sell my company and thereby save heavy legal fees. I notified my attorney to discontinue his correspondence with the other company. During a meeting in Milwaukee with the father and son who owned this other company, I asked for two hundred thousand dollars. After they left, we continued to negotiate by phone and in writing.

Now, I also considered the fact that Randy and Jerri were earning income as part-time employees of Health Staff at our Bloomington/Peoria, Illinois office. A part-time director of nursing was on our staff there; readily available for any nursing care problems that might arise. Randy visited nursing homes to get orders and discussed schedules regarding assignments of nurses to these nursing homes with the office schedulers. Jerri worked out of their house, using her computer to prepare time slip reports used to calculate payroll, calling in the payroll to Paychex, and helping out with each week's billing invoices and recording payments received. Randy and Jerri appeared to enjoy their duties.

Randy Receives Health Staff in Illinois

I wasn't sure if Randy wanted to give up his full-time agent's position with the Prudential Insurance Company. In earlier years, he had thought about starting a business. I thought that if Randy would own and operate Health Staff in his area, he would do well due to his experience in sales with Prudential and earn an excellent income for himself and his family.

I contacted Randy and asked if he would be interested in receiving the Bloomington, Illinois office as a gift. He and Jerri were elated.

Therefore, in my negotiations with the interested buyers, I offered to reduce my sale price from $200,000 to $150,000 providing I would retain ownership of my Illinois company, also called Health Staff, so I could give the Illinois company to my son. The buyers counter offered with $110,000 subject to a signed agreement from Randy regarding his use of the Health Staff trade name in Bloomington and Peoria.

Before the sale was finalized, the buyer's accountant came to Milwaukee and audited Health Staff's books of the past three years. He found that my financial statements and records regarding Health Staff's operations were correct and verifiable. The sale was finalized, and I received the full payment of the purchase price.

Using IRS rules for determining the worth of a business, I calculated Bloomington's value at forty thousand dollars to pass on without incurring any gift taxes or other costs for Randy. I would give all of my company's shares in one transaction to Randy, Jerri, and their children. Randy would be the majority stockholder, and the balance of the shares remaining would be divided equally between Jerri, Jill, and Steve. Randy would be guardian of the children's shares, as they were minors.

I no longer owned the Milwaukee or Bloomington office or was in business anymore. I knew that the time had come for me to retire.

Chapter 27: Happy Times and Sad Times

Whenever Betty and I visited Randy and his family, we slept overnight on their hide-a-bed couch in the family room. We all had fun playing games at the kitchen table, shopping, eating out, visiting special attractions, and so forth. In the evenings, after the children were in bed, Betty and I watched rented movies with Jerri and Randy.

Steve began to play baseball when he was seven or eight years old, and we attended at least one or two of his games each year. We also watched him compete in swim meets. Betty and I also made friends with Randy and Jerri's neighbors.

Diehard Packers Fan

I'm known to be an avid Green Bay Packers fan from way back. I haven't missed a game in person or on television since 1963, the year I returned to Wisconsin from Ohio. The Packers are my team!

In 1978, Betty wrote a letter for me to the Green Bay Packers to be placed on their waiting list for tickets. Ten years later, I received a letter from the Packers informing me I was still on the list, and there wasn't any need for me to contact them, as they would contact me if seats became available.

Then about 1990, Betty called the Packers ticket office in Milwaukee and asked about tickets for the team's Milwaukee games. Because I had been on the waiting list for many years, the ticket agent kindly offered season tickets to my wife, tickets good only for scheduled games in Milwaukee. Our position on the list for season tickets to Green Bay games was not affected. Of course, we were thrilled to accept the offer. We attended each of the two or three games per year played at Milwaukee County Stadium.

In 1995, the Packers organization decided not to play in Milwaukee any more, instead playing all their games in Green Bay. Consequently, each Milwaukee ticket holder was thereafter allowed to purchase special season tickets, called "Milwaukee gold tickets," for two regular-season games and one preseason game in Green Bay. I jumped at the chance to purchase the rights to two regular-season tickets. Betty and I have traveled to Green Bay every year since to watch the Packers play these games.

If the temperature was below thirty degrees, we could not go to the games due to my bronchial condition, which is aggravated in cold weather; and, for sure, Green Bay weather can get very cold. In this case, I would sell my tickets to a registered ticket agent who resold them at a profit. Packers tickets are always in strong demand in our state, subzero weather or not. I heard that there are at least 70,000 persons now on the ticket waiting list.

Before the late 1990s, Randy didn't care to travel from his home to Wisconsin to watch Packers games in person. That changed when Brett Favre became a top quarterback and Randy's son began to take an interest in football.

After the Packers renovated Lambeau Field and added more seats for the 2000-year season. I was offered the opportunity to purchase two additional Milwaukee gold season tickets in exchange for my position on the waiting list for season tickets to all games. With more seats now available, there would be a possibility my waiting list season ticket number could be called in two or three years or so. But, I had been waiting for more than twenty-five years for my number to be called. I thought, "Should I buy two gold season tickets now, for a total of four tickets for three games per ticket each season, or wait for two tickets to all Packers games played each season. Would I gamble two small birds in hand, for one big bird in the bush?

I considered the following: First, at my age of seventy-six, I might not live long enough for my number to be called for full season tickets. Second, it would be a dream come true to take advantage of this offer now so that Randy and Jerri, or one of the kids, and Betty and I could attend Packers games together. I asked Randy, and he was very interested. He was willing to travel six hours from East Peoria to our house and then to Green Bay to watch the team play.

According to Packers' rules, during their lifetime, a ticket holder is not allowed to give or sell his or her season ticket rights to immediate family members or anyone else. Tickets can be passed on to immediate family members only at the time of the ticket holder's death, via a will. Therefore, orders for tickets would be sent to my name and residence.

Due to Randy's increased earnings with Health Staff, I didn't doubt that Randy could afford to pay for the tickets. He sent me the required upfront fee for my two additional gold season tickets. I received his check, cashed it, and sent the money to the Packers. Upon receipt of the tickets, I mailed these tickets to him.

Happy as ever, we attended Packers games together starting with the first preseason game in August 2000. Randy and Jerri came to our house in Harland and stayed overnight. We left early in the morning in one car and allowed two-and-one-half hours for our drive to Green Bay. We attended all three games that year and the next, except I think I missed one November game because the weather was too cold for me. Randy brought Jerri or Steve or Jill with him. In the third year, Randy informed me that he didn't want to meet at our house and stay overnight anymore. I tried to encourage him to come to our house and stay overnight because we had more than enough room. Randy and family had done so for many previous years on their holiday visits. He asked that Betty and I meet him inside the stadium near our seats to visit with one another for a short time because it would be more convenient for him. I did not receive a good reason for him not coming to our house to go together. I was very disappointed.

A Surprise Seventieth Birthday Party

I wanted to surprise Betty for seventieth birthday on January 10, 2002. I arranged a reservation at the Best Western Motel restaurant because the dining area would be away from the entrance, not permitting Betty to see in advance our friends and relatives.

When I made the reservation with the hostess, I discussed the need for a surprise setup, the area to use, and the number of guests. I asked her to contact me personally if necessary. Several days before Betty's birthday, I said to her, "You know; let's go to the restaurant in the Best Western." I had anticipated her response.

She said, "Oh, no, not there! Can't we go to a nice place?"

I replied, "Well, every year for your birthday, I've always taken you where you want to go. Can't you do me a favor this time and go to a place I want to go? Remember when we were there not long ago, how much I liked my steak and you thought your meal was good, too. Come on. OK?"

It worked! Reluctantly, she said, "I suppose, if you want to."

In addition to Randy and Jerri, I invited friends including Keith and Karen Wiest from New Berlin, Tony and Lucille Maglio from Milwaukee, Kathy Liegler and her son, Greg, from Milwaukee, Bob and Laura Chiapetta from Kenosha, Bud and Evelyn Pitts from Union Grove, and Ed Caldario from Chicago.

Two days before the party, I heard Betty on the phone. She said, "You must be mistaken. You have the wrong party. Our reservation is for only two people—my husband and me. What time is our reservation for again?"

After Betty hung up, she told me the Best Western had called and a mistake had been made with our reservation. I waited a short time, then left and drove straight to the motel to see the hostess on duty. I complained about the call because I had left strict instructions not to call our house and to speak only with me. The woman looked at her book and apologized because the hostess who recorded the reservation did not enter those instructions. She entered the information I had originally requested and showed me her entry in the book. Fortunately, Betty didn't even think it was a surprise birthday party for her.

Before we arrived at the dinning area, I had contacted the hostess by phone, and told her we were on our way and to lead us to the dinning area without saying a word. When we arrived, our hostess walked us to the open dinning area. Betty and I walked toward the long tables set up for us with all guests seated, but she didn't show any expression. She wasn't quite looking there and didn't catch on. Then she suddenly noticed and recognized the faces sitting at the table and expressed her surprise as she received a loud applause. The party was a success and a very happy one, and we all had a good time.

After the party was over, I asked Betty, "When we entered the dinning area you didn't show any surprise. Didn't you see anyone or what?"

She explained, "I saw the tables with people sitting there but I didn't look at their faces. I was looking to see where our table was and if we were going to go to our table for two. Then when I looked again, I noticed Keith and Karen, and then it struck me."

I know from past experience with surprises for Betty, at first she is quite stunned and doesn't believe what she sees. Many years ago, when her son lived in California, he and I set up a surprise in which I would take her out for dinner to the famous Pfister Hotel restaurant in downtown Milwaukee and he would show up at our table without any prior announcement after we were seated. While Betty and I were sitting at our table looking at our menus, she with her back to the entrance to the area, Mark walked up to the table behind the waiter and stood in front of Betty. Betty was stunned. She looked at me as though she wondered if she were dreaming. Then she looked again at Mark and knew it was not her imagination! She was so delighted to see him as they hugged each other.

About twenty years later, Mary, her daughter from Texas, and her husband, Richard, wanted to surprise Betty. I brought Betty to the

Forum restaurant near our home for lunch. I secretly kept in touch with Mary by cell phone. While we were sitting at the booth, Betty and Mary were talking to each other on their cell phones as they often do. Of course, Betty thought Mary was at her home in Texas.

In a minute or two, after they ended their conversation, Mary quietly walked to our booth and stood in front of the booth without saying a word. Betty looked stunned, as she had with Mark. She wanted to be sure she wasn't dreaming, she looked at me, and then looked at Mary's face again, and realized it was Mary! Betty was overwhelmed with surprise. Then Richard stepped up and greeted us. We all laughed about the plan's success.

Worries About Randy

At Betty's birthday party, Randy looked somewhat pale and distraught to me. Jerri was looking just fine. I asked him, in a casual manner, "How are you doing, Randy? How's everything?"

He answered, "Fine. OK."

After the party, Betty and I both agreed Randy didn't look good that evening.

A few weeks later, Jerri told Betty and me over the phone that she was worried about Randy because he would be up during the night because he was having difficulty sleeping. She was worried about him because he was not getting enough rest. I decided not to call Randy about this matter but wait until my next visit. On my next visit, he only explained that he wasn't sleeping well. I accepted that Randy didn't want to confide in me.

A short time later, in September 2002, Jerri telephoned to tell me that Randy had moved out of the house and rented a nearby small apartment. Her voice indicated she was very disappointed and distressed.

"Why did he leave, Jerri?" I asked.

She replied that she asked him the same question a couple of times, and he replied that he did not know.

I called Randy and gently asked him the same questions too. He gave me the same answer he had given Jerri—he didn't know. He informed me that he would continue to see the children. I wanted to ask him other questions, but I didn't do so.

Jerri worked part time and knew she didn't earn anywhere near the money it would take to provide for the children. I didn't have any knowledge whatsoever about any financial arrangements between Jerri and Randy. As grandfather of the children, I offered to help provide for the children if needed, but Jerri didn't ever ask me for any funds.

Jerri and I did keep in touch by phone. But when I tried to reach Randy by phone, he did not answer or return my calls. During one of our conversations, Jerri informed me that she expected Randy would start a divorce action against her. I hoped that Randy was doing well in his business, but worried about whether he was earning sufficient income. Jerri expressed the same concern in a conversation with Betty, and Betty suggested she contact an attorney. I don't know whether or not Randy was giving money to Jerri at this time and was not kept informed.

About a month later, Jerri asked me to send letters to her and the children by mail rather than keep in touch over the phone. She did not explain her reason. I didn't have a clue why. Therefore, we wrote to each other. These were warm and friendly letters. Each of the kids also wrote to me. No one referred to Randy or the separation. Then, surprisingly, in the latter part of November, Jerri asked me not to write any more to her or the kids. I was puzzled. I didn't query her.

Jill's Fifteenth Birthday

Betty and I looked forward to visiting Jill for her fifteenth birthday on January 17, 2003. We would also have a chance to see Steve, Jerri, and, hopefully, Randy too.

I telephoned Jerri first, to confirm our visit to celebrate Jill's birthday, because both children were living with Jerri. I wanted to know if Jerri and Randy planned to be together with us for dinner at a restaurant. She informed me that she would not be at the dinner with Randy. Eventually, I did speak with Randy about our upcoming visit. He and I planned that Betty and I would go to Jerri's house first. Then Randy would come over to Jerri's house to pick up the children, and Betty and I would follow Randy to the restaurant.

The evening turned out to be a most disastrous one, having a devastating effect on our relationships. We entered Jerri's kitchen and greeted one another and hugged. I sat in the dinette area with the kids. Then, Betty asked Jerri in the kitchen area if she had contacted a divorce attorney as both of them had discussed in the past. Jerri replied that she had not contacted any attorney. Betty expressed her surprise. Then Jerri became very upset, and replied, "This is none of your business. This divorce is between me and Randy, Jill and Steve!"

Betty immediately walked out of the kitchen and into the living room and stayed there. I was already seated at the dinette table and didn't say a word.

I could see that Jerri went into her bedroom, closed the door, and remained there for the next few minutes. I chitchatted with the children. Then Jerri came out of her bedroom, and the atmosphere settled down. Betty came back into the kitchen. There were no further discussions between Jerri and Betty. We congratulated Jill, and she opened up her birthday present. Shortly before Randy arrived, Jerri apologized to Betty for her outburst.

We left the house, except for Jerri. Randy asked me to follow him and the kids in his car to the restaurant as planned. We were seated and each ordered a soda or drink and our choice of a dinner. For my meal, I had ordered spaghetti with meat sauce. When our waitress brought us our meals, I noticed my spaghetti plate did not have meat sauce but marinara sauce. I politely asked her to replace my dish. She cordially took the plate back to the kitchen, and returned with a spaghetti sauce meal in a jiffy. We had pleasant conversations and a few laughs. We joked with Jill for birthday fun.

As we were leaving the restaurant, Randy asked me if he could visit Betty and me at the motel after he brought the children home. I was thrilled to have Randy come in and spend some time with us.

Randy knocked, and I opened the door. He didn't appear friendly. I sat down in the chair next to the door. Betty was sitting up in the bed away from me. Randy first walked over to Betty and began to speak to her first. His back faced me. It sounded to me as if he was reprimanding Betty about a conversation in the car with Jerri. It is a well-known fact in my family that I don't always hear well, even when using my hearing aids. Unless someone speaks to me facing me, I miss words.

After Randy finished criticizing Betty, he walked to where I was sitting. Now, I could hear every word he spoke. His words have remained embedded in my mind.

He stated, "You have negatively influenced the children and should never visit there again without my permission."

I asked him why and what had I done?

He answered, "You are a negative influence on the children! You complained to the waitress while we were at the table about your spaghetti sauce and then asked the waitress to change the sauce! This is not a good influence on the children." I was stunned by such a remark.

I responded, "Randy, I was polite about it. It's not a big deal. I think everyone at one time or another has sent something back in a restaurant."

Next, he warned me again not to ever come back to visit without his prior permission and suddenly left. I had a sad feeling in my heart and asked myself, "Why! Why did he do this?"

I was not only deeply hurt, but also very puzzled. After some thought, I later said to Betty, "I don't understand why Randy would be so upset over my complaint about my spaghetti sauce. He should be a lot more concerned about more serious matters: How he moved out of the house without explanations, leaving the children with their mother, who was so very worried about her children's future and her future. She was so frightened! He should be concerned about his effect on his children's emotional hurts. I don't know what's the matter with Randy. He just doesn't open up his heart to me or anyone else that I know. Randy thinks he always knows best. It's not good. I would have been glad to discuss his problems with him and help him out anyway I can, instead of listening to his warnings to stay away."

The next day, it was a long drive back home. When we arrived, I telephoned Jerri, hoping she would speak to me. Unfortunately, she would not speak to me then or ever again. I don't know why she was angry with me. I loved her and she had always called me "Dad."

I remain puzzled to this day by Randy's sudden decision to boot us out of not only his life but also our grandchildren's lives. To me, the question of whether to use an attorney for a divorce or a grandparent's decision to return a spaghetti plate for a different sauce are minute reasons to not speak with another person of the same blood. If I had the missing pieces of this puzzle, I would try to put them together to see the whole picture and then try to repaint it.

I have asked myself, "Did I bond with Randy and Lynn?" My heart answers that I enjoyed a strong bond with Lynn starting from the day she was born until she reached age forty-one. I have reminisced often that except for my occasional business meetings out of town, I saw Lynn every day when she was a child, a teenager, and a nursing student; every day until the date of her ma riage.

After Lynn gave birth to Sarah and Lisa, Betty and I babysat for the children. We shared almost every holiday together except on rare occasions. We shared yearly major holidays together and family reunions up to 1995.

When Lynn reached age twenty-four, and I organized NurseCall Inc. in 1981, and hired Lynn, we saw and spoke to each other daily at the office. We went to lunches together almost daily for many years, alone or with employees, until 1990. Then she began to share much of her time with Tom and therefore brought him to most all of our family gatherings.

As with Lynn, I saw and shared time with Randy every day until he reached eighteen and left home. Two or three years later, his employer transferred him to Peoria. Betty and I would exchange visits with Randy and Jerri during their courtship and thereafter. I did not share anywhere near as much time with Randy as with Lynn, however, because Lynn lived in town and we worked together for fifteen years, and Randy lived two hundred miles away.

Randy and I enjoyed a good relationship. After Jerri gave birth to Jill and Steve, we continued to visit them in Peoria and, after they moved to East Peoria. When the children were old enough to travel, then Randy and Jerri came to visit us in Wisconsin, staying for a couple of days, at least, on each one of their visits. We always kept in touch throughout the year and shared holidays until 2002, when Randy reached age forty-five and began to distance his self from Betty and me.

I am disappointed by our current separation, but yet I'm thankful to God to have had these years of wonderful relationships with my children and their children. I hope they will be resumed and we will exchange visits again.

Chapter 28: About Randy

From the day Randy was born, he was a fun child. Movies from his childhood show the toys he liked. One of his favorites was a brown corncob pipe. When he was about age four, he would put it in his mouth and walk around as if he were a grownup. I remember very well how he would stand near me in front of the bathroom mirror in the morning and watch me shave.

Randy and Lynn loved each other's company. They got along very well and rarely fought. I left the office on time each day to be home with them at the dinner table and chitchat. My evening hours were used to interview my clients and prospects regarding their life insurance plans, and to recommend the purchase of life insurance plans suited to their needs. During the weekend, I shared most of my time with the children and Mary Ann. One major reason I didn't accept promotions offered to me with higher wages is I didn't like being away from my family and staying in hotel rooms alone.

When Randy was about four years old, I would play baseball with him. I was so proud of my little son and adored him. His baseball glove was almost as big as he was. Then, in the fall we played football together. I still have a loving memory in my mind of watching Randy run up to the football and try to kick it. Sometimes he missed or hit the side of the football because his legs were too tiny. These kinds of memories are unforgettable.

The funniest family film ever, shows Randy pushing an automobile up the driveway with his "superhuman" strength. Here's how I filmed it. First, I set up my color movie camera on a tripod to shoot only a frame or two at a time. He positioned himself behind the car and placed his hands on the back bumper. He then pushed forward on the car with all his might. I took a shot of this picture. He then moved away from the car. Then I would get into the driver's side and drive forward several inches, stop the car, turn off the engine and return to my camera. Randy would again position himself behind the car and push it for the next shot. These steps were repeated a number of times. The final scene showed Randy pushing and moving the car up the driveway all by himself. That was my son! We had many laughs showing this scene. Randy would laugh as a child when I would tell our guests, "You can see for yourself that Randy is a Superman!"

After we moved back to Milwaukee, Randy began to attend an elementary school named the Thirty-Seventh Street School. It was an old building back then and has been torn down and replaced with Bethune Academy.

When Randy was nine in 1966, we bought a lot and built a new house in the Greenridge subdivision at 12600 West Wilbur Drive in New Berlin, Waukesha County, a couple of miles west of Milwaukee. I was able to do so because I inherited some money, as did my brothers, in accordance with our mom's will.

After we settled in, Pastor Koester of the Holy Trinity Lutheran Church came to our home and introduced himself. He explained Holy Trinity's programs for children and adults to Mary Ann and me. He took special time to describe Sunday school and the three-year, weekly confirmation classes for the children, and invited us to join his church.

Mary Ann and I were impressed with Pastor Koester and Holy Trinity's programs for children and became members. Randy and Lynn attended catechism classes for the full three years. We attended services every Sunday as a family until Randy and Lynn left home. Pastor Koester, who since has passed away, was an outstanding pastor, always interested in the welfare of his church and its members.

Randy's Teen Years

While we lived in New Berlin, Randy attended Frank Lloyd Wright Middle School at 9501 West Cleveland Avenue in West Allis, Wisconsin, and Nathan Hale High School at 11601 West Lincoln Avenue in West Allis. Kids from our subdivision in New Berlin, including Lynn and Randy, attended these West Allis schools because the subdivision was very close to the western border of West Allis. Kids from other areas of New Berlin attended schools in New Berlin. This rule applies yet to this day.

During Randy's teen years, he didn't mix with many kids except three or four boys of his age who lived in our neighborhood. I remember Randy Aschenbrenner, John Cecil, and Dave Dempsey. They all were fine boys. I was proud of Randy for being on the school's track team one year

I knew Randy was searching for his own answers about life's challenges and therefore challenged my views on subjects such as having ambitions, attending college, striving for excellence, earning good grades, choosing good friends, and practicing honesty. In any case, I always tried to discuss matters with Randy to answer his questions the best way I knew how.

One day when he was in his senior year in high school, he noticed I was reading *Money,* a popular magazine for managing money, and said, "Money! That's all you think about—money!"

I commented, "Randy, you have to have it. Everyone needs it. You can't live without it. If you don't have it, you don't eat, Randy."

Of course, I attempted to reason with my young teenage son to help him grow up toward a good life. If he did not get home by curfew time, keep his room in order, or help out with household chores, he would receive a lecture from me. I kept in my mind a sermon given one Sunday by Pastor Koester. In essence, his sermon preached that children are like trees. If a new tree is not pruned and kept straight, the tree would not grow to be strong and mighty.

I only wished to have a wonderful association with my son and guide him to grow up strong, straight, and true. When I was a boy, I know lectures I received from my mother came from her heart. I knew she loved me even if I argued with her at times. But I knew in my heart that she was right and concerned only about my personal welfare.

One of Randy's complaints was that he didn't want to be sucked into the rat race. He said I served as a good example of one who was caught in a trap. I explained my reasons for being in a trap such as the need to work hard, to get ahead, and to earn a comfortable standard of living to avoid repeating the sad years of poverty I had experienced during the Great Depression.

I preached hard about the need to work and to work hard for a better way of life and successful accomplishments—perhaps I preached too much. One day when he restated his argument that he would not get caught up in such a rat race. I asked him, "Well, Randy, what do you plan to do about it?"

He explained, "I plan to move up north, live in the woods, fish, and live off the land." Of course, I hoped he wasn't really serious about pursuing such a lifestyle after he graduated from high school.

Not surprising, Randy didn't ever move up north, or even go fishing that I know of. I smile at the thoughts of teenagers because I don't' recall that we ever ate any fresh fish he caught or vegetables he raised in his backyard.

Randy and College

A semester before his graduation from Nathan Hale High School, I initiated discussion of a full support program for Randy if he would attend Yale or Harvard. I promised to pay for all expenses, books, and tuitions if he would attend either university. I didn't have sufficient funds on hand, but I planned to mortgage our house to pay these costs. Randy refused to accept the offer. Perhaps he had been turned off by the many hours I studied to earn a Chartered Life Underwriter designation while he was a boy.

He did remind me that he would attend the University of Wisconsin in Milwaukee. But, as a total surprise, on the last day for registration, he informed me for the first time that he had made up his mind not to go to college and therefore would not register. All our talks about college during his years in middle school and high school were for naught. I was disappointed. I had never expected that Randy would refuse to go to college. But I was not angry with him. After all, my brother Emil quit high school when he was in the tenth grade, and we loved him the same as always.

The next year, I had a new idea. During a luncheon, I asked, "Randy, if someone offered you a full-time job that would pay you a bonus of two thousand dollars, which you would be allowed to cash after one year's attendance at UWM providing you passed, plus pay for all your tuition fees, books, and living expenses, would you take such a job?"

After he thought about it, he replied, "I would be nuts not to take it."

I said, "Well, I know someone who will do this."

He asked, "Who would do this?"

"Your dad! Will you take it?"

He cheerfully accepted the offer. I nearly jumped up off my seat. Therefore, I wrote out a check payable to him for two thousand dollars. The reverse side stated "Endorsement hereon by the payee is hereby valid after June 15, 1977," the date of his expected successful completion of the first year. I gave Randy the check and he promised not to cash it until next year after passing all his courses. He registered. I paid for his educational costs and living expenses.

Randy completed his first year and passed all subjects. I congratulated him for his fine work and told him he could now cash his check. He informed me at the same time that he had decided he didn't want to continue any further with college. He has indicated to me that he is not an advocate for the need for college. The future will tell whether Steve and Jill will enter a college or university.

Randy and Buddhism

I was very surprised to learn in August 2005, from information posted on his Web site that Randy had organized a Buddhist group in Peoria, Illinois, in November 2003.

To access his site, I simply typed his name into www.google.com. His name, picture, and a brief description popped up. Randy's involvement as organizer, his appeal for new members, and the subjects covered in his meetings impressed me. Randy had not previously expressed such zeal for spiritual development, so I was as surprised as a father can be.

After Randy left home and married, I don't recall him attending church services as a regular practice, though he did attend from time to time. When I learned that Randy had organized his Buddhist group, I mailed a short letter to him briefly referring to his Buddhist activities and asked to let me know if there would be any way I could help him. But he didn't answer.

I've learned some basic precepts about Buddhism using various links on his site. I'm hopeful that if Randy follows the teachings of Buddhism, we will be together as we used to be.

Many of the same principles we follow in Christian religions, such as "love thy neighbor as thyself" and "do unto others as you would have them do unto you," are strong precepts of Buddhism. In my opinion, their precepts are similar in teachings to many of the Ten Commandments. I don't think less of Randy because he didn't continue on with his Lutheran teachings and instead has become a Buddhist, not at all, as long as teachings of love and belief are followed.

Christmas 2004

It was just two days before Christmas, and I thought with holiday hope that Randy would answer my telephone call. On the evening of December 23, he answered my call and my heart jumped. I said, "Merry Christmas Randy! This is Dad." He didn't sound very enthused, but we chatted a while. We talked for almost ten minutes about various subjects. At the time, I hadn't learned yet, that Randy had organized a Buddhist Group and he did not tell me.

He expressed his disappointment with me. He said, "You haven't sent Jill and Steve any cards or Christmas presents for the past three years."

I replied, "Randy, it's really been two years and I would have, as always, but I thought you told me not to visit you anymore, because I had been a negative influence on the children when we were in the restaurant, and I complained about my spaghetti sauce, and I thought this meant the kids too."

But I was filled with joy about Randy's complaint. I was indeed very happy to hear it. Before our conversation had ended, I had mentioned to Randy that whenever he needed me, I was always there.

Betty and I were excited about being able to send Christmas presents to Jill and Steve. As soon as Bergner's, a large department store in Peoria, opened on December 24th, I ordered gift certificates for Jill and Steve to be delivered as soon as possible with a greeting card from Grandpa and Grandma Ruffalo. A pleasant and helpful sales order clerk assured me that delivery would be made to Jill and Steve before noon. When I contacted Bergner's in the afternoon, the store confirmed the gift certificates had been successfully delivered. In addition, I selected two Christmas cards at our local card store and mailed them because late cards are better than no greeting cards at all. I felt the door had been opened!

We received a thank you e-mail from Steve for the Christmas card and gift. But we did not receive a thank you e-mail, letter, or return call from Jill. Then, for her seventeenth birthday, on January 17, I sent her a card with a check. I'm sad to say that she did not call or send us a thank you message for her birthday gift either. I phoned Jill on her birthday and each of the next two days. She didn't return these calls or write to us. In hopes of hearing from her, I later sent her a friendship greeting card and then a discount coupon at Bergner's, but she has not acknowledged receipt. She is now reaching age eighteen, and we are hopeful that she will reflect upon our wonderful times together, get in touch with us soon, and invite us to her high school graduation ceremony in May 2006.

Chapter 29: A Reunion with My Grandson

The Green Bay Packers qualified as a wild card team in the NFL's 2004 post-season play. They would play against the Minnesota Vikings on January 9, 2005 in Green Bay. The Packers don't have enough stadium seats available to accommodate both Green Bay and Milwaukee ticket holders for playoff games. Therefore, to be fair to all ticket holders, the Packers conduct a ticket raffle for playoff games held in Green Bay. For the first time ever, I became a lucky winner of two gold tickets to the playoff game.

I thought I might go, but reconsidered because I was still suffering with my bronchial condition. I wondered if Steve would be interested in seeing this playoff game in Green Bay and whether his dad would bring him to the game.

I sent an e-mail to Steve. It read, "I can't think of anybody else I'd rather give my two Packers playoff tickets to than you. I will be glad to give them to you as a present so you can go, and maybe your Dad or another adult can go with you. I'm also going to send you a letter by regular mail to be sure you get my message." I didn't know if his e-mail address had been changed or even if they read their e-mails.

I also wrote, "The other day I was looking at your report cards that I saved from when you were going to grade school. It brought back many good memories. I'm going to send an e-mail to Jill, too, because I have her old e-mail address, and it (the e-mail address) might still work. I love you, Grandpa. P.S. I'm sure you must be taller now and have grown since I last saw you."

Steve immediately replied, "I would be very appreciative for the tickets. That would be one of the greatest presents I have ever received. I talked to my Dad about it. He said if you did give them to me then he would go to the game with me." Then he wrote about Brett Favre, Javon Walker, and Donald Driver, star players for the Packers, and again expressed that the tickets would be a great gift for him.

I sent the tickets to him by certified mail, with a reply requested, and received acknowledgement of his receipt from the post office. After Steve and Randy attended the game, Steve wrote to me and expressed his appreciation. I hoped with all heart they would have stopped in to see me, as I'm located on their route back home to East Peoria but they didn't.

In the middle of May, after Betty and I returned from Florida where we visited my brother Vince and my old friend Al Bartolini, I tried to contact Steve by phone. When I didn't reach him by phone, I sent him an e-mail. He replied by e-mail a few days later and explained how much he wanted to have a job to be able to earn spending money. But he was not sixteen years of age yet, so he was cutting grass to earn money. He would be sixteen on July 21 and then would apply for work. He did not ask me for any money, but I sent him a letter by regular mail and enclosed a check for a hundred dollars to help him out. He replied, expressing his appreciation and saying that I didn't have to send him money.

In my next e-mail, after briefly describing our trip to Florida, I wrote, "I was thinking about you today, about you being a Ruffalo. You're the young one, and who else is there to carry on the Ruffalo name into the future? One thing we were taught by my mother and father is that we always stick together and love one another no matter what. (Our grandparents lived in Italy.) That we have always done between each other and with our parents. It was a two way street in our hearts."

Meeting Steve in East Peoria

After an exchange of correspondence, I was very happy to meet with Steve in East Peoria. I had stayed overnight in a hotel in Peoria and picked Steve up in the morning at his home.

I hadn't seen him for two and a half years. He had grown a few inches, and his thin body frame was beginning to fill out due to weightlifting exercises with Randy. We had a perfect day together. I'm so very proud of my grandson. He was excellent company and is a fine boy. During the day, I discussed how I hoped I would be able to count on him to visit with us and take care of certain matters for Grandma and me as we aged if we needed him. He appeared to acknowledge he would help, but at his young age, I didn't want to be specific, just let him know he is a very important person in my life.

I asked him at one point, "Are you going to college as soon as you graduate from high school?"

He replied promptly and emphatically, "Oh, I'm definitely going." He said that he was hopeful he could attend the University of Wisconsin, because he considered UW to be one of the finest schools one could attend. He said that his dad was not in favor of his attending UW.

On this visit, I told Steve that I could help him financially when going to college. Jill, his sister, had indicated to Steve that she did not have any plans to attend college. But then later, I heard she would go to a local college in Peoria.

Steve Receives His First Car

I had previously mentioned to Steve that when he reached age sixteen, I would purchase a car for him if his parents approved. He wrote to me that his mom and dad both said that it was entirely up to him. He had his state permit to drive as long as an adult was in the car with him.

Therefore, Steve and I visited dealers in the greater Peoria area looking for a used car to consider for purchase before his birthday in July. He favored either a Honda Civic two-door or Hyundai. He liked a 1999 black Honda Civic two-door in good condition that was selling for $11,000. We had a pleasant mid-afternoon luncheon before I left for Wisconsin.

On the way home, I thought about his car and about auto insurance costs for young drivers. I knew it would be expensive, but I didn't know how much. I had been out of touch with insurance premiums for young drivers for at least twenty years. I knew that he probably would need to be added to his mother's policy to obtain mandatory liability insurance because he lived with his mother and could obtain coverage as a member of her household. Jill lived with her father after her parents' separated and divorced.

I was seriously concerned that Steve's good grades in school could be affected, now and in college, because he would be burdened with paying premiums for car insurance in addition to the repair costs likely with an older car.

Shortly thereafter, Steve sent me an e-mail to tell me that Randy had said the two of them would look for a car in the Chicago area because the deals would be better. If they selected a car for about $10,000 or so, I could send a check payable to Randy so he could purchase the car and then transfer title to Steve.

I answered Steve's e-mail and let him know that I would not send a check to his dad to shop for a car with Steve, because I wanted to have the pleasure of sharing this experience with Steve.

Then, I conjured in my mind that my being in Peoria to purchase a car with Steve could be a chance to see Randy and exchange pleasantries, and also to see Jill, even if for a short time. I wrote to Steve and set up the date for meeting with him to buy his car. I also suggested he ask his dad if he and Jill would come together to pick up Steve's car after I bought it for Steve. His dad could drive it to Steve's house and park it there for several days until Steve turned sixteen and could start driving it. Steve replied and informed me that Randy had something else going on the same day and couldn't make it.

I put my insurance hat on my head again. It had been twenty-five years since I had been owner of my insurance agency. Fathers would often come to my office to discuss their son's or daughter's insurance premiums and the reasons for the high premiums, especially for teenage drivers, and insurance company underwriting rules. Most times, only liability insurance and medical payments were purchased. Collision insurance was considered too expensive.

I contacted two or three agents in Peoria and learned that the premium for liability, medical payments, collision with a $1,000 deductible, and comprehensive insurance on a $9,000 or $10,000 car would amount to approximately $5,000 per year! I thought, "Holy mackerel! It's half the cost of a car six to seven years old with $100,000 miles on it. This doesn't make sense." The collision insurance alone cost $3,000.

I asked myself, "What'll I do now? Shall I pay the entire annual premium? Is it wise to pay $5,000 for collision insurance with a $1,000 deductible on an old car for a teenage driver?" I never recommended such an unwise proposal to one of my clients. There had to be a better way.

I called the American Family Insurance Company, which is licensed in the State of Illinois and Wisconsin, and learned that the cost of the same coverage on a new Honda Civic two-door would be very close to the premium charged on a six-year-old Civic two-door. While I had inquired about the cost of a new car in Wisconsin, I learned that I could lease the car for three years and pay only $200 per month, about twenty dollars less than the lease cost in Illinois. At the end of the three-year period, I would purchase the auto for Steve. My will would provide full payment on the balance of the car in the event of my disability or death.

The annual premium would be $4,900 for full coverage with a $1,000 deductible. My payments would total $21,900 for three years with a full warranty. I felt leasing would be far better than buying a six-year-old used car that would be nine years old at the end of the lease with a cost of $23,500 plus repairs. Why buy a used car? Steve would have zero costs for these items until the fourth year, and then own a three-year-old car. Also, his dad or mom wouldn't have to worry about insurance costs or repairs if Steve didn't have money to pay for them.

Dealers in Illinois and Wisconsin informed me a lease would not be shown in Steve's name even if I personally signed as guarantor of the payments. But to obtain insurance to cover Steve as a driver, the lease agreement would need to be in my name as the lessee in the state of Wisconsin. I called the leasing division of the American Honda Motor Company for U.S. vehicles and learned that there are no exceptions to this rule. I would obtain collision insurance and Steve would be covered as a driver.

I was excited about my decision to get a new car for Steve. During my negotiations for the car, I wrote to Steve and spoke with him over the phone. Then, the next evening, I received a call from Randy. He said Steve didn't want a new car. I began to explain my reasons, but he stressed again that Steven didn't want a new car. So, I agreed to buy him a car worth about $4,000. As long as Steve would be pleased, I was happy too. Randy then ended his conversation with me.

I picked up Steve and we went to visit the Honda dealer at the address shown on the Internet. However, the dealership had moved and their new address had not yet been posted on the Internet. I had brought a list of dealers in the Peoria area with me from home. As we walked to our car to leave, I saw a salesman standing outside in the next lot occupied by a Buick Mazda new car dealer. I asked him if he knew where the Honda dealer had moved. He gave me directions. I told him we were looking for a car selling for $4,000 that I was buying for my grandson.

He thought a while and said, "Normally we take in older cars and sell them at the auction. We don't usually keep them unless we have checked them over and they're in good condition." Then he thought a short while, and said, "Wait a minute, we have a car that's in good condition. It's a 1995 black Nissan that has only 75,000 miles on it. It has a tag on in for $4,900, but I'll see if we can lower the price."

Steve's mother and father each have a Nissan, so Steve was interested! He and I looked the car over carefully. It looked to be in good shape. It was clean, in good shape, no rust or dents, and it tested well when I drove it. I questioned the price. The salesman left for a short time, came back, and informed me they would sell it to me for $4,000.

Then I discussed the sales tax with him and the transfer fee from my name to Steve so Steve would have ownership of the automobile. While the salesman was preparing his paperwork for approval by the sales manager, I explained to Steve that binding coverage would be needed before I would sign my name to purchase the car and transfer the car's title to him. I asked him to telephone his mother so I could explain this to her.

He called her and said, "Grandpa needs to talk with you about something to do with insurance for my car." Steve listened a few moments and told her where we were. After he hung up the phone, he said, "My mom said she is going to call her agent to call you." Her insurance agent called in a few minutes. I asked the agent first if she was a licensed agent with authority to bind insurance coverage for Steve's car. She said that she was licensed, so I gave her the make, model, and serial number.

The car salesman finished completing papers and informed me that the manager, a female in about her late thirties or early forties, told him she would accept the purchase of the car by Steve even though he was a minor, and would include the sales tax payable in the $4,000 price. I considered this a very kind concession. I don't think that most dealers would have accommodated my wishes so readily. Illinois doesn't have a law that prohibits a dealer from selling a car directly to the minor, but for business reasons, dealers normally would not sell a car directly to a minor.

While I was writing my check in the manager's office, I noticed she had the start of tears in her eyes. She said, "You very much remind me of my grandfather, who has since passed away. When I was your son's age, he bought me my first car." I could feel that she was recapturing cherished memories. I hoped that Steve would have good memories of me.

The deal was finished, and I told the salesman that Steve's father or mother would come and pick up the car to bring it to Steve's house. Instead, our salesman drove Steve's car to his house, and another employee followed him to bring him back. I thanked the salesman very much for his help. Then Steve and I went to Applebee's and ate a late lunch.

We conversed about the Packers. Steve had previously informed me that he would be playing football as a wide receiver. His first games would be in the latter part of August. I asked him if he would let me know when he would play so I could come down and he said he would. I brought him home and headed back to Wisconsin while it was still light outside.

I sent Steve a birthday card for his birthday on July 21, and asked him if all was OK with the car. He sent me an e-mail saying everything was fine and he drove the car for the first time on his birthday. Then, in the beginning of August, I sent Steve a note to write back and let me know when he would be playing football. I mentioned that even if he wouldn't play much, I would truly enjoy watching him play anyway. I sent two or three e-mail letters to him; he didn't answer until some time later. He wrote back and apologized for not writing sooner because he was busy working his part-time job and had started back to school. He thanked me for the car again. He didn't address my interest in going to East Peoria to watch him play football. I reminded him in a short e-mail note or two several days later, but he hasn't answered since then. I sent Steve a picture of me dressed in my ensign's uniform during Word War II, but he hasn't acknowledged receiving it. I have left a message on his home phone and haven't heard from him.

Chapter 30: There Must Be a Way

As of February 2006, to the best of my knowledge, Lynn[6] lives in Milwaukee with a second home in Fountain Hills, Arizona. The last news I have about Sarah, from about two years ago, is that she lives in Chicago. Lisa lives with her mother and Tom. Jill lives with Randy in East Peoria. Steve lives in East Peoria with his mother and Mark Cooksey, whom she married in October 2005.

I don't have a clue if Lynn and Randy and families visit or speak with one another. I do know that in most of the prior years, Lynn and Randy's families occasionally visited each other.

Since the days when Randy and Lynn reached their forties and "divorced" Betty and me and all family relatives on my side, I have prayed every Sunday they would end their separation and return to the happy family relationships of the past. I feel that a reunion would be beneficial to everyone, including the grandchildren, for long-lasting memories of grace and goodness.

Many grandparents I've spoken with believe that parents should overlook their animosities toward family members and show forgiveness, love, peace, and harmony as the best answer to strife and separation.

In 2004, I continued to search my mind as to how I should attempt to open discussions with Lynn and Randy. When I discussed these ideas with Betty, she urged me to have peace of mind and stop trying so hard to reestablish a relationship with my children and grandchildren. I wanted her to understand my feelings.

I said to her, "When I'm lying on my deathbed and I ask myself, 'Did I do the best I can to serve as the father of my family, to get my family together?' I want to be able to say, 'Yes, I tried my best.' Honey, I have not reached this point."

She said, "I hope it works out for you, but I don't like to see you be so hurt. You should forget about it. The kids don't care! It's not the same today as it was many years ago when you and I grew up. You know, we would never think about not speaking to our parents."

---

[6] Lynn changed the spelling of her first name to "Lynne" sometime after April 1996. We continue to use Lynn as that is how she has been known to friends and relatives for most of her life.

I meditated for a long time before considering ways to open communication. Would the telephone encourage conversation? I had previously tried calling Lynn and Randy. Each has caller ID and doesn't answer the phone or reply to my voicemail messages. After three or four calls, I'm not desirous of continuing to call and make an outright pest of myself. This option wasn't working.

Would a minister carry my appeal to Randy or Lynn? I recall that many years ago, priests and ministers visited families to help them reconcile their family problems and were held in the highest esteem for their successful efforts. However, I feared that Randy or Lynn would refuse to have any such discussions because they didn't like to discuss religion. I believed it would be very difficult to locate a minister who would be willing to call upon a person not known to be a member of his or her church. But I concluded this method was worth a try.

I began my efforts with Randy. I attempted to obtain the name of a minister through a friend of mine who was a member of a church in East Peoria. I told my friend I promised to make a worthy contribution to the church for the minister's efforts. But, as expected, the minister did not approve because Randy wasn't a member of the church. Therefore, I abandoned this idea. I concluded it also would be difficult, perhaps more so, for a minister to meet with Lynn because she travels back and forth between her Wisconsin home and her Arizona home for business purposes and is unlikely to speak with a minister calling on my behalf.

Would a social worker or psychological counselor contact Randy on my behalf? Years earlier, after Lynn had resigned from my company and I couldn't see Sarah and Lisa anymore or speak to them, I had contacted a family counselor in Waukesha County, Wisconsin, where Lynn lived at the time, to arrange for me to meet with her. Lynn did not want to proceed with any mediation efforts. So, I thought to hire a private counselor and to start again with Randy.

From Milwaukee, I called a counselor with a doctorate degree in psychology who practiced in Illinois. I explained my dilemma to him and asked for his recommendations. He graciously offered to help me, but suggested that he should first call Randy and attempt to arrange a meeting with him. He contacted Randy at his office and called me. He explained, "I called your son at his office and introduced myself. I gave him my name and my profession. Without saying a word to me, he slammed the phone in my ear. I'm sorry, Mr. Ruffalo, but I don't think there is a thing I can do for you."

Still, I was not going to give up because I did not have a doubt in my mind that my intentions with my son and his family were righteous, without enmity or animosity. We are taught to love thy neighbor as thyself and certainly our parents, sons, and daughters. I do not harbor any animosity or feelings of estrangement toward my son Randy.

I have often thought, "There has to be a way! Would a detective who could visit Randy on my behalf work for me as my intermediary?"

I knew from using investigators in the insurance industry and my healthcare company that detectives are not shy, and go almost anywhere in their efforts to satisfy their clients' needs. I hadn't ever hired a detective for personal reasons, but I was running out of options to make contact with Randy or Lynn.

I didn't have anywhere else to turn. Lynn and Randy didn't speak or associate with any of my family or friends. I didn't have a friend in the world I could contact to intercede on my behalf.

I hired a detective in East Peoria two year's ago to contact Randy, and one in Milwaukee to contact Lynn. After providing background information to these detectives, I stressed to each of them, "I'm hiring you because I have only one goal in mind and that is to get my family together and for you to open the door to communications. I'm eighty years of age. This matter is very important to me."

My detective in Peoria met Randy at his home and spoke with him in person in November 2004. Randy promised him he would write a letter explaining why he didn't speak with me. He agreed the detective could pick it up to forward it to me. I waited about three weeks. Since I hadn't heard from my detective, I called him. He informed me that he hadn't received the promised letter and would visit Randy again at his house and then call me.

He contacted me in two or three days and reported Randy had apologized to him for not having his letter ready and said he would write it for sure. The detective could pick it up. It never happened.

In our short phone conversation on December 23, 2004, about Christmas presents for Jill and Steve, Randy confirmed to me that a detective had been to his house and came back to pick up a letter, but Randy hadn't given him one.

My Milwaukee detective contacted Lynn a few days before Christmas 2004, and appealed to her to meet with me during the holiday season with a warm heart and love. He was an emotional man. He reported to me as follows: "I finally did reach Lynn at her office. I told her, 'It's Christmastime, and your father would like to meet with you. He loves you very much and wants to talk in person with you.' When I told her this, she sounded cheerful and laughed a little. She said she would think about it."

Lynn didn't ever call the detective or me.

Soon, I decided to travel to Peoria and find and meet with a professional counselor in person, explain my story, and seek his help to arrange a meeting with my son. I knew if I were able to contact Randy personally, he would not speak with me.

On a day in the latter part of November 2005, I arrived in Peoria about ten in the morning and used the yellow pages to write down a list of a few psychologists. My calls from my home in Franklin hadn't worked out very well. I had a difficult time getting around Peoria because I didn't know the city, and there was heavy freeway construction. Although I have a navigator in my automobile, it didn't help me due to heavy construction on major streets in Peoria.

Finally, I found the psychologist's office. He was alone in his office, very busy, but said he would speak to me for a few minutes. I explained to him those events that led to Randy's shutting Betty and me out of his life and about the spaghetti sauce incidence. Before talking anymore, he wanted to place my name and address in his records. I said, "Sam Ruffalo."

He said, "Ruffalo?"

I answered, "Yes, that's me."

"I know a Randy Ruffalo," he said. "Is he related to you?"

"He's my son! How do you know him?"

"I meet your son every so often in the bank downstairs and we say hello to each other. His office is across the street."

"I didn't know that! I knew his office was on Sheridan Road, but near where his mother lives. I don't know Peoria very well."

He told me that he would call Randy, speak to him, and then contact me in the evening if he had been in touch with Randy. I received a call as promised.

The psychologist reported, "Randy told me that he was not happy with you and your wife because your wife had an argument with his wife on his daughter's birthday (on January 17, 2003, when Randy and his wife were separated prior to their divorce). He came to your hotel room and complained to your wife that she should not have argued with his wife about having a divorce lawyer, and you sided with your wife."

I immediately replied. "What? Wait a minute. I did not hear what Randy said when he criticized my wife. He had his back to me. I didn't have any knowledge of what he said. I'm hard of hearing and wear hearing aids. Unless someone is speaking directly to me in front of me, I don't make out the words very well. I thought he was complaining to her something about a conversation while in their car. I only know that he faced me directly when he complained to me about my sending the spaghetti sauce back in the restaurant as a negative influence on the children. I heard this message, but not anything else."

The psychologist suggested that I write a letter to Randy and apologize. He said he would review my letter before I send it to Randy at no charge. After I wrote it, he returned it to me, stating that I should include an apology. I called him and explained I didn't know what to apologize for. If I knew I would apologize. I sent a Christmas card to Randy and wrote on it that I was very proud of him as a father who is showing he is concerned about the welfare of his children.

As it stands, in July 2006, my last conversation with Randy was in July 2005 regarding my purchase of a car for Steve's sixteenth birthday. I have hopes that Randy will desire to watch the Packers play football and to bring Steve with him to the games, but with Grandpa too. Our house is on the way.

***

Life's harmonious family relationships are priceless.
Voiceless family relationships are worthless.
—*Sam S. Ruffalo*

Final Thoughts

How Do I Feel About Where I Am Today?

Having grown up well versed in the restrictions and sadness caused by poverty, I would say I'm satisfied with my current financial situation. Over the years, my multi-faceted business career has enabled me to earn an increasing income to reach a net worth in excess of one million dollars. Such financial security is invaluable to my wife and me. It provides a comfortable standard of living, access to adequate medical care when needed, and peace of mind that we will always have food and shelter, without having to toil on our hands and knees, even if the country suffers another economic disaster comparable to the Great Depression.

Unfortunately, a man's true wealth cannot be measured in just dollars and cents. Yes, we have enjoyed the country club atmosphere, affluent neighborhoods, golf, travel, extravagant dinners, and social affairs. But what we most cherish, what we truly value, are the good times spent throughout our lives with our children, grandchildren, family and friends during holidays, birthdays, summertime gatherings, weddings and many other family events. Many of those good times are gone now, leaving an empty place in our lives and our hearts. We do not believe we deserve our children's separation from us, and pray it will not last.

Cherishing the Past

A lifetime of faith in God and belief in the endurance of family will continue to feed my hope that my family can overcome past differences and be whole again. I know my mother and two brothers and I would not have survived the hardships of the Depression without our resilient family bonds. Our family, as it was then, our relatives and friends, will always be remembered for their spirit of love and helpfulness, and for their faith in humanity, always looking for the light that shines upon us, never seeking the darkness instead.

I'm proud of the work we did back then. We didn't know self-pity or unhappiness despite our impoverished lifestyle. We were wealthy in other, more important, ways. We had our love for one another and the joy and happiness of sharing true friendships with our relatives and friends. Materialism was not the order of the day. Strong family bonds and friendships overcame any hardships, except illness, and provided us with a wealth of rich, rewarding experiences. Neighbors loved one another, expressing concern and respect for one another and a willingness to be helpful in times of distress and need. These memories shine as a bright light over the somber times of sadness and poverty.

Believing in the Future

Since the end of the Depression, our country, overall, has enjoyed increasing prosperity. Although many Americans enjoy a better economic life, there remain poor people who need help. There are, as well, people who need to help themselves by showing some initiative and taking advantage of the many opportunities that exist in our nation. Today, people in many households struggle with their financial pressures not for necessities like food, shelter, clothing, and medical care, but for luxuries such as larger homes, advanced communications and entertainment systems, high-end automobiles, and extravagant vacations. There is a vast difference in the motivation driving Americans today verses those who lived during the Depression. Where people once worked to survive, they now work for comparatively excessive comforts.

Then, as now, there remains a vast rift between the poor and the wealthy, the haves and the have-nots. Despite this persistent disparity, I truly believe our nation still provides opportunities for both groups. The have-nots need to pursue their goals with hard work and application of their best efforts. There are no shortcuts, no tricks outside of a good conscience and strong ethics. After my time in the service during World War II, I had decided to become one of the "haves." I was unsuccessful in my first business attempt. I had failed. But I kept trying, constantly striving and working hard to succeed in my continuous efforts to fulfill my dreams. I did not ever think of giving up.

I hope there will be those who read this story and are inspired to make their own dreams come true. After eight decades, I've learned it is important to have a strong desire and the will to win, determination, perseverance, belief in yourself and faith in God, and the love and joy of sharing your life with family members for a splendid journey of long lifetime memories.